I0147685

AVID
READER
PRESS

YOUR LAST FIRST DATE

Secrets from a Hollywood Matchmaker

Jaydi Samuels Kuba

AVID READER PRESS

New York Amsterdam/Antwerp London Toronto Sydney/Melbourne New Delhi

Avid Reader Press
An Imprint of Simon & Schuster, LLC
1230 Avenue of the Americas
New York, NY 10020

First Avid Reader Press hardcover edition January 2026

AVID READER PRESS and colophon are trademarks of Simon & Schuster, LLC

Interior design by Ruth Lee-Mui

Manufactured in the United States of America

1 3 5 7 9 10 8 6 4 2

Library of Congress Control Number: 2025945692

ISBN 978-1-6680-7964-5
ISBN 978-1-6680-7966-9 (ebook)

To the family I came from, the family I chose, and everyone who's allowed me to play a role in helping them shape theirs.

Contents

Introduction xiii

Preface xix

ACT ONE

CHAPTER ONE
The Inciting Incident
"You're my last hope."
3

CHAPTER TWO
Once Upon a Time
"A partnership was born."
11

CHAPTER THREE
The Leading Man
". . . I was convinced his inner Romeo was in there, somewhere . . ."
19

CHAPTER FOUR

Scene One, Take Three

"'That horrible date just cost me a thousand dollars . . .'"

29

CHAPTER FIVE

The Meet-Cute

"*. . .* how *you meet your forever partner is far less important than meeting them at all."*

43

CHAPTER SIX

The Fatal Flaw

". . . not all sparks are good—sometimes they light a tree on fire and burn down an entire forest."

51

CHAPTER SEVEN

Pride and Prejudice

"Singles I actually *consider 'picky' typically fall into one of two categories: insecure or delusional."*

65

CHAPTER EIGHT

The Conflict

"'Let's just call it red flag territory *. . .'"*

75

ACT TWO

CHAPTER NINE

Here's Looking at You, Kid

"He was in touch with his feelings, but perhaps not the right ones at the right time."

89

CHAPTER TEN

Building Character

"Who am I to advise them on their dating lives when my own love life is in shambles?"

95

CHAPTER ELEVEN

I Wish I Knew How to Quit You

". . . right now, your profile could use more personality."

103

CHAPTER TWELVE

The Midpoint (AKA The Inevitable Step Backward)

". . . I don't think the right man for you will make you cry. At least not this early, and this often."

119

CHAPTER THIRTEEN

Location, Location, Location!

"Was their poor connection really a result of my restaurant choice . . . or had they been a doomed match from the start?"

127

CHAPTER FOURTEEN

The Hallmark Vacation

" 'That woman wouldn't know passion if it were grabbing her in the rain outside a rowboat in South Carolina!' "

137

CHAPTER FIFTEEN

The Inner Monologue

" '. . . I don't believe most daters are manipulative or undesirable candidates for partnership.' "

143

CHAPTER SIXTEEN

The Hollywood Montage

"The only green things I love are money and emeralds."

159

CHAPTER SEVENTEEN

The Light Bulb Moment

"A person on the receiving end of a breakup can react in one of two ways: they can break, or they can break away."

169

ACT THREE

CHAPTER EIGHTEEN
The Antagonist
"I'd laid out the perfect road map to happiness . . . and there she was, choosing to ignore it."
179

CHAPTER NINETEEN
Recovering from Heartbreak
"You can't beat yourself up for one mistake forever."
185

CHAPTER TWENTY
The Climax (AKA The Last First Date)
". . . I'd always fantasized about being the lead in my own rom-com."
197

CHAPTER TWENTY-ONE
The Leads Learn Their Lesson, Part One
"'. . . he didn't understand why I wouldn't instantly melt when he'd bring me flowers . . .'"
203

CHAPTER TWENTY-TWO
The Leads Learn Their Lesson, Part Two
". . . it's a widely held belief that our most toxic trait is the direct opposite of our primary love language."
209

CHAPTER TWENTY-THREE

The Predictable Ending

"Perhaps the key was to have it all . . . a little bit at a time."

221

CHAPTER TWENTY-FOUR

The Resolution

". . . she was beginning to truly love herself—

the only guidebook she really needed."

229

CHAPTER TWENTY-FIVE

The Denouement

"To celebrate the joys and—let's face it—to troubleshoot,

we'll always have each other."

237

CHAPTER TWENTY-SIX

The Hollywood Ending

"While I don't think heartache is an inevitability,

it doesn't have to be in vain."

243

Acknowledgments 247

Introduction

As a six-year-old kid in South Florida, watching Billy Crystal belt clever musical parodies onstage way past my bedtime, I dreamed of winning an Oscar one day. (That vision stuck: my bat mitzvah theme was "the Academy Awards.") But even as I continued to fine-tune my acceptance speech, I never imagined I'd be matchmaking some of the nominees one day instead.

Working in the entertainment industry for several decades, I became a fly on some pretty glitzy walls. Whether I was a guest on an A-lister's private jet or watching forbidden bonds form on rainy-day movie sets, I learned that the people I admired most in life were exactly that: people—and this meant that most of them, like the rest of us, struggled with their dating lives. And no matter how many blockbuster films or accolades they'd accumulate, it seemed that in the absence of romantic love, they concluded that their lives were devoid of meaning and purpose.

I didn't notice this initially, because I was too busy attending networking events or attempting to prove my chops in a male-dominated, cutthroat environment that required the majority of my attention. But as I accumulated TV credits, and survived some pretty toxic writers' rooms, my professional dissatisfaction started creeping in. At the encouragement of friends, I started a matchmaking "side hustle," born from my natural instincts to help connect people—and the parallels between it and my day job quickly became apparent.

To craft compelling characters as a writer, I had to dig deep to figure out what made them tick. The same held true for matchmaking, except in that case, I was dealing with real people. I soon realized that introducing one happy couple would bring me ten times more joy than penning the 250th episode of *Family Guy* ever would (and I admit, that brought me a *lot* of joy). That's not to say I'm not proud of my writing accomplishments, but when I think about how I want to be remembered one day, it's not for penning fart jokes for Liam Neeson: it's for helping people find their forever partners, the ones they're comfortable farting in front of.

I'm not the first matchmaker in Hollywood. (A mutual friend supposedly set up Prince Harry and Meghan Markle on a blind date, and Ed Sheeran introduced Courteney Cox to her musician partner, Johnny McDaid.) I'm just one of the first to do it professionally. Over the years, my clientele has ranged from high-powered studio execs and actors to Emmy Award–winning writers, former child stars, and even celebrity body doubles. But I've always been a firm believer that love should be accessible to everyone, and my diverse database reflects that.

In this book, I share insight into three clients' journeys with me—each a composite of several I've worked with over the years. I've also changed various names throughout to protect confidentiality. Choosing whom to highlight was difficult, because to some degree,

I'm invested in every client I work with. My excitement is palpable when they have a mind-blowing first date, and so is the pit in my stomach if they get their heart broken. But I must admit, I connect with some more than others. (Any coach who claims complete objectivity is, at best, fooling themselves.) In my case, I'm most drawn to people who share my same driving force in life—for some that might be success; for others it's fame; and for still more, it's having a good time. But for those who've jumped for joy in college dormitory stairwells following an intense first make-out session, or sobbed hysterically singing along to Keane's "Somewhere Only We Know," our driving force is love.

Whether you're the hopeless romantic, the one in a rush to "make it happen," the one who's convinced yourself you'd be better off alone, or even the one who's "figured it all out" but wants to play matchmaker for your friends, my hope is that you'll recognize yourself in these stories. If you're lucky enough to have already found your forever partner, you'll relate to the journey of my clients and instantly be transported to the time in your life you feared you might wind up alone. And if you're in that headspace now, you'll learn more about who you are, how you fit into the dating landscape, and what more you can do to achieve your desired result.

Like in some of the best movies, a spoonful of sugar helps the medicine go down. (The sugar in this case is the journey of me and my clients, and the medicine is the actionable tips and tricks you'll realize are suddenly in your arsenal—the effect of ten one-on-one coaching sessions with me—by the time you're done reading this book.) I also use these characters as vehicles to address common dating dilemmas everyone can learn from. Given my background, I'm savvy about the mixed messaging pervasive in the dating industry—one I was also exposed to before I met my husband. For instance, should you hold out for someone who checks all your boxes, or should you settle for someone else "good enough"? Should you bring up politics at the beginning of a date to help gauge someone's values, or avoid the topic altogether? Should you sleep with someone on night one, if you're feeling it, or wait until you're dating exclusively? I'm here to tell you, like with all your other burning questions, *it depends*. I understand why witty catchphrases and universal rules and charts are appealing: it's tempting to follow every get-love-quick method if you only complete steps X, Y, and Z. But when it comes to dating, I've found that what works for one person might completely repel another—and this nuanced philosophy is reflected in my coaching style, and in these pages.

I also hope to foster empathy for "the other side," or some of the "offenders" you've dated—the ghosters, the catfishers, the love bombers, and those darn singles who simply won't commit. As someone who has coached many of those men and women, I shed light on why they might act the way they do. And if you're guilty of some of these behaviors yourself, perhaps reading about the effect they have on hopeful singles you come across will cure you of these bad habits once and for all.

In addition to sharing insights about various types of daters, I also analyze the rising popularity of matchmaking (in part due to popular films and dating app burnout). I not only illuminate the perks of investing in such a journey, but also expose some bad industry practices to help guide you toward selecting the perfect matchmaker or dating coach, if that's what you're in the market for.

Some people believe that's AI. Founders and CEOs of major tech companies have suggested that AI bots will be able to provide superior coaching one day, whether it's for use within the unique ecosystem of their apps, or even lessons applicable to in-person dating.

While I recognize the merit of AI's involvement in the dating sphere, I don't think it—or even the world's best human dating coach—can top your own experience, education, and intuition, should you choose to start relying on it. The best dating coach, in my opinion, isn't someone you can turn to for advice, but someone who enables you to start trusting the advice you give yourself. This is a mindset I hope all my clients will eventually adopt, and one I hope to impart to you, as well.

To trust the advice you're about to receive, though, I'd also like you to get to know me. Some coaches make a point of not getting too personal with their clients, but I find that providing a glimpse into my own life, whether it's a win in the present or a mistake from my past, helps to normalize a client's experience and allows us to better connect—something I'd like to do with you. I'm eager for you to know more about me and my dating history, what inspired me to get into the matchmaking business (and eventually the date-coaching one), how I created my company, why I structure it the way I do, and how all this led me to the happy marriage I'm in today. Not everyone can get high on their own supply and marry their client (more on that later!), but if I can achieve my "Hollywood ending," I know you can too—whether you're an A-list celebrity or movie set extra.

Preface

Squirming uncomfortably in my hospital bed, I looked around the room filled with several new faces and wondered whether they were judging me. When I had purchased my custom-made medical gown off Etsy, I'd thought the blue and white abstract pattern would help take my mind off my anxiety. I'd known today was coming for a while, and hoped to don something other than the ill-fitting, depressingly bland covering standard for such experiences (clearly a common thought given an entire category on the shopping platform is dedicated to such garments). I'd even gone so far as to find out the specs of "normal" hospital gowns to ensure that my creative alternative would get approved by staff. But as I lay outstretched on the hospital bed like a chicken waiting to be spatchcocked, it occurred to me that my thoughtfully procured, stylish getup was doing very little to ease my growing discomfort.

Several pairs of hands maneuvered around my body, tearing off elastic strips and pressure-sensitive gauges that had been monitoring my vitals, and I did my absolute best to disassociate. *Dave will be back any minute to help calm me*, I told myself. *Or maybe he'll miss this procedure entirely (although the nurses did claim it "couldn't hurt" for him to visit the cafeteria—a place, I'm now learning, where all cell phone reception goes to die). Will* I *die today?* The thought crossed my mind as the masked-up strangers started wheeling me out of the room.

"He'll be back soon. Don't worry," a nurse tried comforting me with an upbeat tone that felt strangely out of place given the urgency of the situation.

I felt the medical team quicken their pace as they continued ushering me toward the operating room. I was feeling a little faintish, which the clairvoyant nurse seemed to clock. She attempted to distract me.

"Is it true you're a matchmaker?" I think she asked. (I say "I think" because I was so doped up on narcotics that I can't be sure.)

"Mm-hmm." I nodded politely, scanning the hallway for my husband.

"Wow, amazing," she continued heedlessly. "So what's, like, your craziest matchmaking story?" I shielded my eyes from the light as the double doors to the operating room swung open. "Anything you can share?"

The last fifteen years of my professional life flashed before my eyes. Over time, I'd collected dozens of zany, ridiculous, hard-to-believe stories that I kept at the ready for this exact kind of question, but as I braced for one of the scariest moments of my life, I didn't find myself thinking about my most outlandish clients at all. Instead, I thought about some of my favorite ones—all of whom I'd worked with until not too long ago.

ACT ONE

THE INCITING INCIDENT

I wasn't in a nineteenth-century shtetl, conspiring with a woman's friends and family to arrange the perfect marriage for her, nor was I a third-generation matchmaker, born with the road map to love coursing through my veins. Rather, I was a self-trained dating expert, sitting in sweats in my home office, still trying to figure out the basic mechanics of Zoom.

It was 2020, and I was about to meet my newest client, Callie, on the recently popularized platform. As I waited for her to appear on-screen, I admired my background, which didn't always look so professional. The built-in bookshelf behind me displayed a wide array of relationship and self-help titles from gurus I admired (and loved to critique), along with an assortment of endearing trinkets my husband and I had accumulated over the years, including a framed Shakespearean quote, colorful Cuban cigar boxes, and a replica of a

WWE wrestling belt—a remnant from Dave's bachelor life I generously suggested we keep.

The curated setting was appealing to prospective clients, but the truth is, I much prefer relaxing on my comfortable but awkwardly low custom couch in the corner of the room that sports a blank white wall behind it. As a writer, I never really feel creative or productive at a desk, and find that the same holds true as a dating coach. Clients also respond better when it feels like we're just two friends gabbing away on a sofa. But Callie was a new client, and I wanted to impress her. I thought about hiding Dave's wrestling belt for a moment, but decided to leave it be. It was usually a good conversation starter.

When I noticed Callie's name in the waiting room, I ran my fingers through my ponytail and plastered on a welcoming smile. I was in my usual getup: dressy on top, casual below, a virtual matchmaker's equivalent of a mullet. I quickly shrank the Zoom screen to fit beside the profile I'd created for Callie, so I could seamlessly glance between the two. The standard information was hardly a comprehensive road map to what makes a person tick or what they're looking for in a partner, but it allowed me to skip some of the basics during our conversation.

Name? Caroline "Callie" R*****

Your age? 42

Height? 5'4"

Sexual orientation? Bisexual (though I've mostly dated men).

Where do you live, and what is your living situation? I own a two-bedroom condo.

Where are you from, and where else have you lived? Providence, Rhode Island. Philly for college.

What's your profession? TV studio exec.

Race or ethnicity? White.

Religion? None but I was raised Protestant.

Your political views? Liberal. Trump is infuriating.

How important is it for you to marry someone of the same faith? Not. Prefer someone spiritual over atheist though.

What is your highest level of education? Undergrad at UPenn.

Most serious relationship and when/why did it end? My ex wasn't ready for kids.

Do you want and/or already have kids? I do, and froze my eggs a few years ago (thanks, WB insurance!).

Please describe your type, if you have one: Smart, funny, slightly corporate, successful, loyal, likely still reads the newspaper. Into finance types. Someone who has a passion for what they do for a living, or even a hobby. I dated this guy once who was obsessed with a flight tracking app, and he was able to identify planes based on their silhouettes. That's hot.

Do you have any dealbreakers? No one unemployed or aspiring, bald, or short. Absolutely no one with birds, and definitely no exes (will share more in person)!

Please list your hobbies: Playing violin, pickleball, skiing, going to concerts, traveling, listening to podcasts, brunch with friends. I'm also weirdly good at throwing axes.

Tell me something about yourself not listed above. It's okay to brag: I was in *Forbes*'s "30 Under 30." I'm also a former high school sailing champion.

"Hi!" Even over video, Callie was clearly stunning: sophisticated with stylish, short hair—how I would have pictured Audrey Hepburn if she'd been in a rock band. There was a darkness to her energy, but she also exuded a calm confidence as she waited for me to speak.

Small talk is usually my business partner Lauren's thing ("small talk, big connections," she liked to remind me), but she was currently on maternity leave. Without her, I could sometimes start off a bit awkwardly. ("Nice to meet you. I'd love to hear more about the cult you escaped as a child.") This time, I stuck to her playbook and asked Callie how she knew Anna, an assistant director and former client we matched successfully, who referred Callie to our service. I always ask how close a connection is, in case there are any overlaps in possible matches. (I once played a role in two friends' falling-out—all because I'd accidentally introduced them to the same man. Avoiding this requires some sleuthing, but hey, I don't need any more blood on my hands!) Callie informed me she and Anna were merely work friends, and suggested they had different types anyway.

"No offense to Marc," she offered, referring to Anna's boyfriend.

I found talking to Callie to be easy. I learned that after graduating from UPenn, she'd moved to LA with the goal of working with actors. She started at an agency but quickly fell in love with TV development, and wound up accepting a job at a major studio. The youngest executive in her department, she dedicated the majority of her late twenties and thirties to her career, with pretty impressive results—some of my favorite shows in the last decade, it turned out, were ones she'd helped shepherd to screen.

She was happy, but one day she'd woken up and realized she was alone. Most of her friends were married with kids, and she found herself longing for permanent companionship. She'd thought that if she treated dating like a job, she'd eventually find that special someone, but after several dead-end courtships and some good laughs on Raya, she had grown dissatisfied with her prospects. And she was determined not to settle.

Based on her questionnaire, I already had several men and

women in mind for her, but first I had more to discuss, like what age range she was open to. We landed on 32–52, which gave me plenty to work with.

"But let me ask you a question," I threw out there. "If I meet someone fifty-three, who otherwise fits what you're looking for, do you want me to categorically rule them out for you? Or would you want to at least grab a drink with them?"

She replied that she'd want to grab a drink, so I pressed for her actual limit. I don't do this to test people, but rather to ensure I'm not accidentally ruling out someone's future husband or wife based on a birthday. Age ranges are useful on dating apps, when you know little else about a person and are conducting your own search. But the benefit of using a matchmaker is we can help flag any outliers for you.

I rattled off a few other outstanding topics: Was she down with someone who already had kids? Since she wasn't politically active, was she open to someone else who might be? What about someone who does mushrooms twice a year in the desert? After Callie responded to everything with ease, I was feeling hopeful—no, *excited.* She seemed to know what she wanted, but was also open to someone else outside of that.

"I feel really good about this." Callie smiled effortlessly as I continued to pick her brain. "I looked into doing IVF, and I mean, I'll go ahead with it if you can't find my person, but it would be so much better to have a kid with someone else, don't you think?" I wasn't sure whether she was asking rhetorically, so I waited. "You can make that happen for me this year, can't you, Jaydi?" she suggested, half jokingly. "You're my last hope."

I froze, feeling both honored and horrified. For years, I strove to be a beacon of light for those struggling to date in a difficult landscape—dating is tough anywhere, but in a city like LA where people are self-absorbed, pursuing their own passions, and constantly searching for the "next best thing," knowing where to find a quality person looking for something real is tough—but never had I thought of myself as anyone's "last hope."

"When you say 'this year,' do you mean by December?" I questioned, feeling panicked.

"No, no," Callie reassured me. "I mean the end of *my* year. With you."

The distinction wasn't much better. A year is a good amount of time to find someone's match, but the consequences were greater here if I failed to produce one. We weren't talking a possible membership renewal, or another round of online dating, if the One failed to materialize. We were talking about Callie pursuing motherhood. On her own. I felt the knots tightening their grip on my stomach. I was already incentivized to find her someone great, but this added challenge felt like a veiled threat. The last thing I wanted was to compromise on quality for her as a result of added pressure or guilt.

What's more, Callie had no idea how personally her request weighed on me. Dave and I had been struggling to conceive for a while, and finally, after resorting to IVF ourselves—after what felt like endless needle pokes and procedures—I was technically seven days pregnant. (At least, I hoped I was. The more reliable blood test to confirm it all was in four days.) I'd tried imagining many times what my own journey to bear children would look like without Dave by my side, and every time, I'd come to the same conclusion: I wouldn't want to do it alone. If Callie couldn't find her partner in time, would I be partially responsible for her shouldering that burden?

I took a deep breath and reminded myself that I'd "solved" harder cases. Her declaration of intent had caught me off guard, but ultimately, I admired her resolve. (I actually know many people and former clients who've expanded their family through fertility assistance—at least four single women and one single man—but hadn't been an instrumental part of their IVF journey since it took place before or after their memberships with me.)

Callie was forty-two, and statistically, her window was closing to make her dream of having a biological child a reality. She was willing to do it alone if she had to, and it was my job to honor that possibility. What's more, I liked her. Clients might benefit from their therapist maintaining a certain sense of detachment in order to remain as objective as possible, but my job was to be *subjective*: to use my experience and instincts to help make meaningful connections happen. It was only natural that the more I got to know a client, the more invested I'd become in their journey. And the more invested I was in their journey, the more motivated I'd be to hunt down every possible lead for them.

Fortunately, Callie had also signed up for date coaching. The majority of my clients come to me wanting the "quick fix" solution of having their husband or wife handed to them on a silver platter. But this implies the table is already set. Callie seemed to have her act together, but experience told me there was more to her relationship status than a string of bad luck. Before diving in with her, I planned to conduct a routine "health and wellness" check on her dating life to get a better handle on her history and confidence level. I also needed to dig deeper on what type of partnership she was seeking. Did she want something more traditional or modern? Did she envision herself with a spender or saver? The list went on.

As I scheduled our next meeting, I could sense Callie's renewed optimism. She was smart. She was successful. She was determined. And, in that moment, I decided I could help her.

ONCE UPON A TIME

As a heartbroken freshman in college, I didn't plan on becoming a matchmaker. But as I struggled to overcome the grief of being blindsided by my high school sweetheart, I realized I couldn't stay away from love for long. While I had trouble finding it again for myself, that I was a natural wingwoman was obvious to everyone else around me (e.g., if my shy best friend spent two hours doing her hair and makeup only to freeze when the hot guy at Les Deux approached her, I was the first to make conversation on her behalf). It never occurred to me I could turn that into a business, though. Instead, my sights were set on the place where all love stories originate—at least, the epic ones starring Ryan Gosling: Hollywood.

I'd known I wanted to be in the film industry since childhood, and even shot a documentary on my high school campus called "Behind the A+," featuring four seniors competing to be valedictorian.

I should have recognized my true calling back then: the characters I was most interested in were the handsome, intellectual jock and brilliant, under-the-radar theater nerd, who had separately confessed in interviews that they were crazy about each other. They wound up dating, thanks in part to my encouragement off camera.

I never finished that documentary, but I did get into USC film school. I didn't realize it at the time, but nearly every script I wrote there centered around a love story. While most students were letting off steam at frat parties and spending summers abroad, I was peddling my free labor to whichever talent manager, production company, or studio would have me. I figured if I made the right connections, maybe those love stories could get made some day.

Shortly after graduating, I got hired as a production assistant on *Family Guy* and quickly sensed a trend in the office: it seemed that despite living their professional dreams, nearly every woman over thirty who worked there was single or unhappy in her relationship. What felt like week after week, a particularly adorable and tenacious coworker I admired would come into work crying. She was the whole package, who wanted nothing more than to meet the man of her dreams and start a family, but even though she was putting herself out there regularly, she was still meeting really low-quality men. The few good ones she did meet lacked follow-through. *If someone this sweet, fun, and accomplished is having trouble meeting the right guy*, I thought, *how will the rest of us fare*? I was convinced all she needed was an introduction to the right man, and I decided that I could be that connector. From there, my matchmaking side hustle was born.

At the start, my introductions were fairly incestuous. After all, I could only set up people I knew. Recruiting strangers made me uncomfortable—my worst nightmare was that some suave, good-looking bachelor I approached at Erewhon would join my database and later go on to do something untoward to one of my friends or trusting clients (a hypothetical later explored in Celine Song's film *Materialists*), so I stuck to referrals or people with mutual contacts I felt comfortable enough "inviting." Absurdly, I named the company LJMatchmaking: "LJ" for "Lady Jaydi," a cutesy-sounding nickname that inadvertently likened me to a madam (eventually, I was able to repurpose the "L" to stand for my business partner, Lauren).

I started out charging a nominal fee, which only seemed fair given my lack of experience. But while most straight women were willing to pay anything necessary to help navigate a tricky dating scene, the handsome, successful, and down-to-earth men they wanted to meet were skeptical. In fact, most didn't want to pay at all! They believed they could easily score quality dates on their own, and paying someone else for "help" in that department was a bruise to their egos. So I adjusted. Instead of requiring men to pay *me*, I insisted they pay for their dates (which most were doing already anyway). This system allowed the women to invest in our company, and the men to invest in our women. Before long, I had an enviable group of bachelors at my disposal.

For years, I juggled the company on the side while racking up writing credits—starting with *Family Guy* and *Salem*, and then eventually developing my own content with producers such as Jennifer Garner and Margot Robbie. (Some curious coworkers knew about my matchmaking side hustle; others would have been shocked to learn I was squeezing in client meetings and scheduling dates between writers' room sessions.) To my surprise, the two careers started to complement each other, and I was even drawing inspiration from some of my clients for work. These story ideas ranged from the tragic and heartwarming to the aspirational or even comedic, like how one client would only accept first dates days 9–15 of her menstrual cycle, when men are scientifically proven more likely to find her attractive, or when another client walked out on his date because her brown hair reminded him of his schizophrenic mother.

I was making a good living writing at the time, and decided to run LJM almost like a nonprofit, simply charging so I didn't incur losses. In addition to complimentary memberships for straight men, I offered the same to LGBTQ+ singles and women over fifty, since I felt I didn't have a deep enough database to justify charging them. Fewer than half my clients were actually paying me! Anyone with half a brain for accounting would have quickly realized that this model sucked. (For comparison: in LA, the average rate for matchmaking is ten thousand dollars for eight matches; in NYC it's fifteen thousand. Some elite ones are even known to charge between a hundred and five hundred thousand. Three Day Rule's global million-dollar white-glove experience even comes with a custom-designed engagement ring.)

But I believed in the art of matchmaking as a means to find love, and wanted it to be accessible to everyone. By prioritizing client success over profit, my patience paid off. I started making more and more successful setups, and was able to build up membership and increase my rates, without compromising the integrity of my mission. This mindset wasn't only good for my clients; it was good for me. It allowed me to operate in volume—more clients and database members meant more potential matches to make. By 2014, I'd set up a good handful of phenomenal couples, and word was beginning to spread.

Then I met Lauren, an unscripted producer and a cofounder of a group called Hollywood Women Executives Stronger Together, aka Hollywood WEST. She wanted to go into matchmaking, and was already aligned with the general practices of my company, such as keeping all the setups blind. (I'm all about organic first impressions.) She ultimately believed that joining forces with me would be more effective than launching a competitive business of her own, and pitched me her services at a Hollywood WEST function. Almost immediately, I brushed the idea aside. Although my database was increasing, the workload was manageable, and I enjoyed the autonomy of making all the matches myself. I explained to her that my database wasn't big enough to justify any help. What Lauren heard was: "If you can make my database larger, I'll *need* your help." And that's precisely what she did.

I lost track of the number of referrals she sent my way, and eventually it made sense to collaborate. At first, I suggested she only sit in on meetings with the clients she herself had scouted, but as business progressed, I realized she couldn't effectively weigh in on their matches because she was unfamiliar with the rest of my database. So, I eventually had her sit in on *all* intake meetings, and quickly discovered I enjoyed bouncing ideas off her. Our commonalities brought us closer, but our differences, more than anything, made us a great team. Lauren was the blonde to my brunette, the logical thinker to my bleeding heart, and the Miss Piggy to my Liz Taylor ("two of the most iconic and beautiful Hollywood history figures," according to Lauren). We were both driven, resourceful, community oriented, generous in our friendships and romantic lives, and enjoyed matching people overall: with roommates, jobs, and, of course, love.

A partnership was born.

As it turned out, Lauren was more than a great personality fit. She also had the brains for business that I hadn't quite developed yet. She reminded me we had an LLC to create, tiered membership rates to name and structure, a website to design, and many more tedious but practical steps on the journey to help quality singles find "the One."

She also kept my naivete in check. When I first took a stab at matchmaking, I thought it would be simple: match Person A with well-suited Person B and *boom*. Cue the engagement rings. What I didn't account for was that just because someone wants love doesn't mean they've done the work necessary to achieve it. Lauren also forced me to admit that some people are harder to set up than others, sometimes for reasons out of their control—and they need to be considered differently when it comes to promises and results. Women over forty who want children, single parents, men with roommates, someone insecure about their body type: most of them will make incredible partners, but when clients treat matchmaking like a trip to a Build-A-Bear workshop ("I'll take young, busty, outgoing, and blonde, please!"), it can be a tricky medium.

So, how could I help everyone while still making a profit? With Lauren's guidance, I started thinking in terms of mutually beneficial outcomes, and we introduced a waitlist. Rather than take on any dater willing to pay, we would only activate someone's membership if we felt, ahead of time, that we had enough potential matches for them. This helped maximize our success rate, but more important, it didn't make anyone feel duped after signing up with us. It also made the overall process that much more rewarding when we were able to successfully match someone from a more challenging demographic—like a late-sixties divorcée.

Still, I didn't want to leave the bachelors and bachelorettes on our waitlist hanging, and eventually, I came around to the idea of coaching. Celebrity matchmaker Patti Stanger, introduced through a mutual connection, was the first to suggest I try it when we met at her monochromatic beachside home in Marina del Rey in 2018. She was everything I expected from her public persona and more. Quirky with a flair for the dramatic, she encouraged me to consider date coaching in addition to matchmaking, as you can achieve more immediate success through it (and, depending on your rates, it can be more lucrative). I already had a primary source of income writing TV on top of my business, and wasn't sure I wanted to add more to my plate. *Besides*, I thought, my impostor syndrome at its finest, *who am I to tell someone else how to date differently?*

But as time went on, I heard so much feedback from men and women following their dates—both good and bad—that I started to feel confident in the insights I was gaining from the secondhand experience. At some point, I told myself I was doing a disservice to clients *not* to intervene and suggest adjustments on their behalf, if only they were willing to listen. I slowly rolled out a coaching arm to my company, and it didn't take long for me to recognize the joy and fulfillment I received from those sessions. As extensive as my matchmaking database was, I could never guarantee someone's future husband or wife was in it. But with coaching, I had the opportunity to achieve 100 percent success. Whether I was helping singles up their flirt game, revamp their online dating profile, or adjust their nervous dating habits, I knew I could improve someone's dating life after just one session.

Now, I wasn't just squeezing in client intake meetings and scheduling dates between writers' rooms—I was also conducting full-blown date-coaching sessions. I was having trouble figuring out what to focus on. A podcast Lauren and I were guests on, *First Round's on Me*, wound up helping me decide. We were there to talk about dating in Hollywood, and at one point during a rapid-fire round of questions, we were asked to participate in a little ol' game called "Fuck, Marry, or Kill." I waited for options.

"Entertainment industry, dating coaching industry, and Jason Momoa," the cohost Steve Rossiter threw out playfully (Jason was a callback to an earlier conversation—let's just say that Lauren has a hall pass).

"I'd definitely kill Jason Momoa," I began somewhat morbidly, without missing a beat, "hook up with entertainment, and marry date coaching." I caught my breath for what felt like ten seconds. The host quickly moved on, but I was shook by my certainty.

I'd found my calling.

THE LEADING MAN

While I'd been in a good headspace following my meeting with Callie, one phone call with my fertility doctor changed everything. As with our first round of IVF—and the devastation that followed—our doctor had no scientific explanation for the failure. "You just have to try again," she'd told us calmly, as if the concept of implanting another possible life-form in my body was the same as trying a new Pilates class. I started to wonder whether my end goal of getting pregnant was even possible.

I considered canceling my sessions for the day, but I knew that out of all my clients, Kent would be an enjoyable distraction. He hadn't been connecting with any of the phenomenal women I'd introduced him to so far, which was frustrating, but my conversations with him after all the ill-fated dates were so entertaining that I almost didn't mind. He even invested in a membership upgrade, which came with access to a wider pool of bachelorettes, including former clients and acquaintances who weren't yet enrolled in the service. It also covered date coaching. He initially insisted coaching "wasn't necessary," but came around to the idea when his ego got the better of him (he had to know how a woman had perceived him, even if he wasn't interested in dating her). This type of curiosity always amused me. If he wasn't interested in her romantically, what did he care how she thought of him?

Over time I stopped sharing specific feedback with clients. I'd been burned too many times by those who used my honesty as ammunition, such as when a rejected attorney angrily texted his match, perturbed she'd complained to me how often he brought up his ex. "*You're* the one who asked about my dating history!" he vented. If a client's behavior is consistent, though, and can't be traced back to one individual, I feel comfortable intervening—especially when that behavior is preventing them from making a meaningful connection. ("You have a tendency to bring up your ex on dates, and it's turning women off.")

I couldn't tell how much value Kent was getting out of our sessions, since he usually did more talking than listening, but for whatever reason, he kept coming back for more. I'd been working with him in this capacity for a few months now, and nearly had his "stats" memorized.

Name? Kent M****

Your age? 58

Height? I'm 5'8" on dating apps

Sexual orientation? Straight.

Where do you live, and what is your living situation? Own my house in Eagle Rock, where I share custody of my 2 kids every other weekend.

Where are you from, and where else have you lived? Born in NJ but raised in NC, lived in the South for a bit before moving to CA.

What's your profession? Film director, investor, and vineyard and winery owner.

Race or ethnicity? Nothing exciting.

Religion? Jew-ish.

Your political views? Middle of the road. Socially progressive. Would probably vote for any minority at this point just to move the dial.

How important is it for you to marry someone of the same faith? Would make my mom happy, but she's been dead a long time.

What is your highest level of education? Bachelor's.

Most serious relationship and when/why did it end? Does anyone really know?

Do you want and/or already have kids? Happy with the 2, but with the right woman, who knows?

Please describe your type, if you have one: Self-assured, independent, early riser, positive. Someone with a sparkle in her eyes. Should look decent in a bikini.

Do you have any dealbreakers? Jealous types, gold-diggers.

Please list your hobbies: Biking, hiking, nature, horseback riding, time with my kids, I also play piano and drums. Always looking to try something new.

Tell me something about yourself not listed above. It's okay to brag: As a director, I've won multiple awards. But I'm most proud of my wine label. Oh, and I don't own a TV.

Scrolling through his profile again, I smirked, recalling the clearly dated headshot he initially attached, as if knowing what he looked like a decade ago would somehow overshadow any impression I'd have of him now. I'm always puzzled by clients who feel the need to send unsolicited photos of themselves, given that my company, in part, is known for its blind dates. Besides, whatever filters they use on their online dating profiles are wasted on me. The instinct for someone to misrepresent or de-age themselves speaks volumes, and those who do it usually wind up being especially looks-driven in their search, expecting to punch well above their weight class. Kent was a bit of a "silver fox," if you went by his matches' feedback, but he did look his age and refused to entertain a woman in the same category. He claimed he wanted to settle down but treated matchmaking like ordering off a menu. He whined about not connecting emotionally with the bachelorettes he was meeting on his own, but rejected the smart and successful women I recommended who would address that very issue.

Still, I felt invested. Despite some misogynistic humor, he could be extremely intelligent and charming. And while he wasn't especially vocal about his romanticism, I was convinced his inner Romeo was in there, somewhere—otherwise, why would he bother taking the time to meet with me so regularly? In a way, his self-assuredness and personability reminded me of my husband, and perhaps that's why I was so motivated to help him. But he didn't make it easy.

I almost always meet with clients in person or on Zoom, since so much can be gleaned from facial reactions and body language. But Kent had been in postproduction on his latest movie, and let me know he'd be phoning me from his office during his lunch break. I was eager to address the callous recaps he'd been sending me following his recent dates, which—while admittedly entertaining—failed to steer me in the direction of a more suitable match for him.

Kent was surprised when I broached the subject, claiming his feedback had been "pretty clear" so far. I pulled up some examples, hoping that by repeating his words to him, he'd realize the frivolousness of his superficial generalities. I started with his thoughts on a woman, Kate:

"'I found her cute and attractive. Almost an "8." I did not, however, feel a distinguishable need for carnal knowledge.'"

Kent chuckled amusedly. "See? You got where I was going there."

"Svetlana," I powered through, determined to make my point. "'Not sure I wanted to bang her. You should feel comfortable setting her up with others, though. She's a cool chick.'"

I waited for what I thought would be a semblance of acknowledgment. Instead, he seemed pleased by his "generous" description. I moved on to Astrid, whom he called a "9."

"You didn't feel like 'mauling her face,' though, you said. You see what I'm getting at?"

There was silence on the other end of the line.

"When we first met, we agreed that physical chemistry is important. Even *necessary*. But you're giving me nothing else to go by," I complained to him. "Did you find these women funny? Smart? Did you open up to any of them?"

"Jaydi, Jaydi, Jaydi." He laughed jovially, as if he were the one giving me a lesson on dating. "None of that matters if I'm not feeling attracted to them."

"Okay. But '8's, '9's . . . these are objectively beautiful women you're meeting here." Even as I said it, I winced. Assigning numbers to women based on their looks is a common practice, but one that I abhor. That said, I'd never ask Kent, or any other client, to adjust their language with me, because hearing their uncensored thoughts is usually the best way to gain insight into their mindset. Something about the numerical classification triggered me, though. And then I realized: it reminded me of the grading system for embryos.

In what is also a subjective process, embryologists assign letters to embryos based on their potential for development. Without knowing what's going on genetically, they go by how embryos look. What I'd learned, though, is that grades have little to do with the outcome of a transfer: embryos that appear inadequate often work without a hitch, and ones that look great in a lab often possess defects invisible to the naked eye—evidenced by the life-form my body just rejected.

Similarly, when it comes to a person's appearance, other qualities such as personality and energy can really shape how attractive they appear to a partner. Studies show that confident and outgoing women are generally perceived as more attractive than more muted versions of themselves. I wasn't sure how much Kent factored this in, but he should've known better. After all, how many "10"s had he dated only to discover that he didn't enjoy spending time with them? And conversely, how many incredible women had he connected with in person, whom he categorically might have rejected online? I asked aloud whether he was focusing on the right things.

Kent insisted he wasn't as "picky" as I thought, so I suggested we try narrowing down his preferences more in the looks department. Was he more into sweet or sultry? He said he could go either way. When it came to height, he declared he was "pretty open" there too. I felt my eyebrows subtly rise. *Pretty open* was not how I'd define Kent, but I pressed on, inquiring about curvier body types. (When we first met, he shared that he typically dated more petite women.)

"I'm a boob guy, but I have my limits," he added. "Curvy how?"

"I don't know. Curvy but fit. Take Kate Upton, for instance." I threw out the first name that came to mind. "Would you kick her out of your bed?"

"Who's Kate Upton?"

"Okay," I chortled, adjusting for our generation gap. "What about Kate Winslet?"

"I doubt I'd kick *any* woman out of my bed," he responded hastily. "The question is: would they make it there?"

I stifled a smile. "Okay. So why didn't these other women 'make it there'?"

At first he worried about the optics of "putting someone down," but he got over that fast. "Since you asked, Jaydi, and I guess it's helpful for you to know: Kate's voice was distractingly high-pitched, Astrid wore too much makeup, and there's no way Svetlana would feel comfortable at a black-tie affair, which I have to go to sometimes. You know, for work."

"So Astrid wore *too* much makeup, but Svetlana doesn't wear enough?" I repeated back to him, making sure I understood his distorted logic.

"She's not feminine enough for me. I prefer long hair and a natural essence. Kind of like Darla."

And there it was. A week had passed since I'd first introduced him to Darla, a curly-haired and dynamic makeup artist I'd started working with recently. His written feedback about her was actually the most positive yet, and I was excited to dive into their date. He'd decided to meet her over a happy hour, which wouldn't have been my first choice (for a while now, I'd suspected he had been double-booking himself, as his dates were feeling rushed). But according to both parties, his date with Darla went well.

I glanced at my notes, armed with Kent's colorful description of the evening. *"Darla was great. We shared a talk-time ratio of 50:50, which was really nice. Talked about you and your business a little bit. All good. Question: she said that her friends are comprised of people who have 'shared beliefs and shared experiences.' I heavily gravitate toward people who have friends from all walks of life. Might be a mismatch for this reason. All said and done: very sweet and engaging person. I'd have made out with her, but not in the 5:30 p.m. stink of Hollywood."*

Perhaps now he'd buy into my reasoning for scheduling dates later. Statistically, I always have more success when they're scheduled after seven, and the data supports that. There's an increased feeling of intimacy and romance at night, when there's typically fewer distractions, and let's face it—the lighting is better! Women report feeling more confident when blemishes and imperfections are masked by the moonlight, or the forgiving dim of a restaurant's warm lighting, typically used at night to create the feeling of a more relaxed atmosphere. There's also a hard out, if it's needed, or a natural transition to a sleepover.

I wondered whether he was planning to see her again, and he shocked me by nonchalantly revealing they'd already had two more dates since the first. I couldn't believe it.

"You buried the lede, Kent!" I grinned, intrigued. "You must really like her."

"Nah," he said, somewhat dismissively. "My ex just had the kids for the weekend. Darla's great, but I don't think we have enough to talk about."

As he explained that he didn't plan to see her again, I wondered how to pivot. Kent often tried to elicit reactions from me, and I wondered whether that was happening again here. If I pushed him to continue seeing her, he'd likely resist. But if I glossed over his blatant dismissal of her, he'd probably see through it.

Instead, I decided to capitalize on his good spirits and ask if he'd be open to some "wildcard" introductions. I'd given him the "best" of what he'd asked for, and now I wanted to try things my way, like having him meet someone closer in age.

Normally I had to be careful with clients when broaching the idea of expanding previously agreed-upon search parameters. Often, the suggestion of doing this triggers feelings of insecurity or failure. Many people don't believe they deserve what they're asking for in the first place, so the moment you challenge them to consider alternate options, they worry that you don't believe their asks are attainable either. I would never want a client to lower their standards, though. Instead, I liken the concept to ordering fish at a restaurant. The majority of people request popular fish, such as salmon or cod, which are lower in mercury, and typically reside closer to the ocean's surface: fewer explore the bottom-feeders with migrating eyes and inferior mouths. But sometimes, those are the tastiest! And by trusting, let's say, a seasoned sushi chef (or matchmaker), that omakase experience might introduce you to a fish you'd never have tried, but that you'll be salivating over thereafter. If only I could get that through to Kent.

"Don't worry," I assured him. "I know your taste."

"Okay," he offered finally. "But if she ain't sushi-grade, I'm sending her back to the kitchen."

SCENE ONE, TAKE THREE

“They kicked you out too?” The woman across from me was still grumbling about PayPal to one of our colleagues.

“Yup,” the colleague replied. “These credit card processing companies claim matchmaking is too ‘high risk.’ ”

“I’m telling you, just go with Square, girl. You can build the fees into your pricing.”

I shifted in my seat, wondering whose side conversation I’d be able to join naturally. Today was the third time I’d attended an unofficial assembly of dating professionals, and once again, I was left wondering whether it would be worthwhile. The woman who organized the first, May—founder of Two Asian Matchmakers, a company seeking to help men aged 35–65 meet Asian women—created the meetups as a collaboration tool. But in a way, these gatherings—typically held at large tables on restaurant patios or in conference rooms—have become a place for us to vent about industry challenges, size up our competition, and inflate our value enough that our peers will feel comfortable referring hard-to-match clients to us.

That day, I had one of my own, and I was determined to find a possible bachelor for her. While it's standard industry practice to tap competitors for referrals, I almost never do it, as my own database is usually extensive enough. But in this case, finding a compatible man for the bachelorette I was working with had proved to be more challenging than usual. Aly, the raven-haired cofounder of Matchmakers in the City (MITC), a premium company I consult for, took a sip of her drink beside me. She had just wrapped another conversation, so I took advantage of the opportunity and pulled up a photo of my client Meera. (While my dates are typically blind setups, when I'm collaborating, pictures are a necessary tool and always kept confidential.) I shared more about Meera and watched as Aly racked her brain in consideration.

Aly'd started her Beverly-Hills-based matchmaking firm years ago with her sister Cristina at the famous pool where the cast of *The Hills* was discovered. Without producing "evidence" of prior success, she and her sister brazenly approached singles there and asked whether they'd be interested in signing up for their services. The budding entrepreneurs threw out a fee of a few thousand dollars, believing that the costly rate would make their company sound more exclusive. It worked, and their business has grown exponentially since.

"I've got two perfect guys for her." Aly smiled. "I'll have Anthony email you."

Carina, a kindred spirit nearby, wondered if she could see the photo too. As a dating coach, Carina was known for adopting a nurturing approach with her clients, rather than exerting tough love.

We'd initially met working for MITC, but forged a professional friendship as we bonded over our own respective operations on the side. Hers, called Atlas, mostly serviced people based in international hot spots such as London and Dubai. With her beautiful curves and understanding eyes, she was instantly disarming to males and females alike. (She was also the most patient dating coach I knew, so if Carina ever declared that a client was "beyond help," I believed it to be so—at least for the time being.)

"She looks sweet," she commented on Meera's photo. "I might have someone for her too."

We were about to chat more when a familiar, singsong voice broke the low hum of conversation. "Sorry I'm late!"

Melody. Accompanied by her iconic blonde hair extensions and signature skinny jeans and stilettos, she entered the patio, apologizing to everyone for running behind. (Apparently, she'd just left the set of an unscripted TV show she was contributing to.) The fanfare surrounding one of our region's "It" matchmakers was typical, but I was both envious and annoyed. I felt Melody was more style than substance, at least when it came to looking out for her clients.

Her website touted her as a sought-after matchmaker "to CEOs and celebrities alike," yet a mutual acquaintance and former coworker of hers confessed to me he'd only ever met one high-profile client in the four years he'd worked for her. Almost immediately, the bombastic blonde had everyone enraptured as she talked up her latest bachelor: a six-foot-five Russian attorney who exuded some of that "strong but toxic masculinity." She solicited referrals as she continued describing him, and I couldn't believe how many of my colleagues were jumping at the opportunity. It was as if, through her outgoing nature and magical fairy dust, she was hypnotizing everyone to believe this domineering and problematic guy was actually a "catch."

When the conversation settled down, our fearless leader, May, took out her clipboard and kicked off the introductions. Energy healer and "soulmate connector" Marla went first. The award-winning author and life coach focused on matching affluent men, and always brought positive energy to these get-togethers. I was happy to see her and waved a small hello. Next was Dana, my senior by almost two decades, and our group's "Real Housewife," as I liked to call her. Perfectly coiffed and decked out in designer wear at all times, she loved to remind us of the business she was constantly turning down—what we "ladies" needed to do, she insisted, ignoring the fact that we weren't all ladies (Barry, the lone male dating coach, was listening silently in the corner). She told us that her life changed completely when she stopped taking on the clients she didn't want to work with. She then went on to brag about a new technology she'd been given access to that would "revolutionize" the industry, she claimed—but when given the opportunity to elaborate, she said she couldn't reveal any more details without first discussing them with her attorney. When she was done, attention shifted to Kristy from D8able, who specialized in upping clients' curb appeal, tackling everything from overall style to their hair and household. As she talked, I made a mental note to try to chat with her later; I knew several clients who could probably benefit from her expertise. Carina went next. And then, it was my turn.

"Hi, I'm Jaydi," I started clearly. "I'm a cofounder of LJMatchmaking, which specializes in setting up people in the entertainment industry. They call me and my business partner the 'Love Agents of Hollywood.'" I smiled self-consciously. The title, originally bestowed upon us in 2018 by Ari Berkowitz, a TV writer and former client of ours, was a memorable moniker, but I always felt uncomfortable using it to "sell" myself.

"Is it true you set up half the cast of SNL?" A redheaded woman I didn't recognize jumped in as she leaned toward me, curious.

"We've had some clients who've worked there," I replied to her honestly. Her question caught me off guard, as it's an unspoken rule that everyone's database is confidential, unless we choose to disclose it. "But if I tell you who, they might have to impersonate you on the show." The woman gasped, and I couldn't tell whether she was amused or offended.

"I heard you set up Kendall Jenner once," another piled on. I channeled a stoic expression from my time as a competitive tennis player, back when opponents called me "The Silent Annihilator." I'd never set up Kendall, but figured there wasn't any harm in a little bit of intrigue.

May suggested the prying woman, Bianca, go next. From her muted, couture pantsuit, it was clear she worked for one of our industry's giants. While many of us ran smaller boutique agencies, companies like hers, akin to It's Just Lunch or Tawkify (which had managed to create a presence in every state), claimed to "scale the art of matchmaking"—something that felt contradictory to me. Through their models, numerous matchmakers operate in every city they service—often employees who "look the part" but lack the necessary experience. (Many are even passionate about exploring our field, but I'm passionate about singing in the car, and that doesn't mean I should be headlining concerts.) In those scenarios, Matchmaker A might get to know his or her client well, but the strongest match for that person might have been interviewed by Matchmaker B. I admire what these companies have managed to accomplish, but I prefer matchmaking in its purest form. This means personally getting to know every one of my clients and those I match them with. It's why I mainly operate in one city.

Normally I refrain from discussing philosophy with representatives from those companies, to avoid confrontation and to focus more on the ways we could collaborate. But then, I heard it. "Six hundred couples and counting!" Bianca touted her success rate, shrugging as she did so, as if throwing out a number like that was at all normal or realistic.

"You've introduced six hundred couples who've gotten *married*?" I asked, trying to mask my skepticism. I was eager for her explanation.

"Well . . ." Bianca backtracked. "At our company, we define 'success' by first dates."

"Meaning first dates that lead to *relationships*?" Melody joined in, equally curious.

"Meaning . . . first dates that lead to second dates." *There it is*, I thought. *The stats that "trick" unsuspecting singles to invest in their service.* I could hardly blame Bianca. After all, she couldn't help it if that was how her massive company decided to frame her work. Still, if we all went by those metrics, some of our numbers would be in the thousands. Bianca lowered her eyes, embarrassed. I felt bad calling her out, but the comment felt too egregious to let slide.

While she was guilty of displaying more naivete than malice, I wondered whether prospective clients were aware of the potential repercussions that could occur as a result.

Most people start a dating company because they're passionate about helping people find love. Matchmakers can do what computer-generated algorithms cannot: meet countless individuals, face-to-face, and determine who is most worthy of their clients' time. But once profit enters the equation in this over $4.1 billion industry, the business side of the business can wind up overshadowing the desire to help people. I've heard some of my colleagues refer to matchmaking as a "luxury service," and in some ways it is. But this sentiment likens having a matchmaker to owning a Ferrari or Hermès purse—all seen as "status symbols." While we indeed are providing a luxury experience, I strive to make finding love "affordable" for everyone, and structure my business model accordingly.

Not all profit is evidence of abuse, though. Some business owners who specialize in matching wealthier clientele are phenomenal at their jobs and justified in charging whatever they see fit. After all, the time, effort, and skills required to help procure one of the world's most important and precious commodities, love, deserves compensation (and has been rewarded for centuries—in Judaism, *shadchans* are entitled to a brokerage fee by Jewish law, and *nayan* in India might even receive clothing, food, or farming assistance in exchange for their expertise).

But there's a fine line between being properly compensated for all the vetting, convincing, recruiting, and scheduling required to make meaningful connections happen, and taking advantage of a vulnerable population willing to pay whatever it takes to find their forever partner—something some bad actors have been known to do. When a matchmaker starts off "too big, too soon," that's more likely to occur. Before having a sizable database to match people from, some matchmaking company owners jump into hiring employees, opening a brick-and-mortar location, and taking on additional, somewhat unnecessary expenses in order to appear more credible. Then, they pass those costs down to their clients, finding creative ways to justify their steep rates. Aside from the actual matchmaking, perks such as photography sessions, wardrobe consultations, mock dates, wingman or wingwoman services, coaching sessions, and more might be offered. The thinking is that even if you don't meet your forever person through paying for one of these services, at least you'll gain perks as a result.

There is truth to this logic, but some in our business use perks as a shield to deliver subpar matches. Contractually, a match is usually considered "quality" if two people are on the same page about marriage and kids, and other common deal-breakers involve religion or politics. But additional important factors such as looks, income, social skills, and more are often considered subjective. In sales meetings, prospective clients are assured their preferences will be honored; however, it's rare for any one matchmaker to have enough men or women in their database who will meet all of a client's expectations. (Even if they did, there's no guarantee those database members are looking for that client back.)

So, what happens if a company has three high-quality and realistic contenders for you, but you were promised eight? Where do those five other guaranteed matches come from? Often, matchmakers will turn to their competitors for a standard $250 referral fee (which is a helpful incentive, but less ethical matchmakers will knowingly refer an inferior match simply to collect the referral money). There are also traditional forms of recruitment at singles' events, country clubs, or white-collar networking functions. There's even a "matchmaker's matchmaker"—a firm called "Match Resource"—that companies can hire to help track down other possible leads for you.

These options are great, and can sometimes connect you with your future husband or wife, but other times, companies are doing what you could be doing yourself, for free: scanning social media apps, such as Instagram or LinkedIn, to find dates, even surfing dating apps using manufactured profiles—which can lead to married, mentally unstable, unemployed, and other "undesirable" people populating some databases. Rumor has it that one male matchmaking employee even poses as a "hot girl" on the internet to lure in unsuspecting bachelors. While matchmakers who employ those tactics might get points for creativity, do you really want to shell out thousands of dollars for matches you could find yourself online? If you're a wealthy professional who doesn't wish to be "bothered" with the search, the answer might be yes. If you've chosen to invest in matchmaking at the expense of other life choices such as freezing your eggs or sending your daughter to private school, possibly not. More virtuous matchmakers will turn down clients attempting to hand over more than 20 percent of their income.

Personally, I avoid guaranteeing a minimum number of matches to anyone. I prefer to focus on quality, and instead have clients sign up for a window of time. When a client pays for a guaranteed number of matches, if even one introduction is off base, they might start calculating the "cost" of that match—for instance, "*That horrible date just cost me a thousand dollars,*" an attitude that causes even the most gifted matchmakers to be more risk averse. By avoiding this trap, I'm more easily able to throw in some "wild card" matches who might be perfect for a client, but outside the realm of what they "requested."

Clients aren't the only ones paying for matchmaking. If you can't afford the steep rates for such a premium service, database memberships are almost always offered instead (a lesser tier where you aren't actively being matched, but rather considered as matches for higher-paying clients). This can be a worthwhile investment when the pairing is mutually beneficial, but that isn't always the case. For example, a male client in his seventies may "request" a gorgeous forty-something database member who wasn't previously open to such a wide age gap. A more seasoned matchmaker will level with that client during his sales meeting, letting him know when an ask like that is unrealistic or less likely to be fulfilled, and share reasons for needing to expand the search. But a less experienced matchmaker might make the requested introduction anyway to satisfy the higher-paying member, and that can result in a disappointing experience for the person in the database.

Before deciding whether or not to pay for a database membership, consider whether you know someone who's already had a good experience with that company. I'd also take geography into consideration. If a firm's main headquarters are in the South, for example, don't pay their database fee if you're in Milwaukee. This may sound like a given, but some companies misrepresent their reach. When possible, try finding a local matchmaker based in your area. After all, as Lisa Purdum, the CEO and founder of Love Inc. Matchmaking, once told me, "Proximity is power."

Finding the right matchmaker for you might be tricky, but investing in that person can change your life. So what are some questions that can help you recognize the good ones? "Are you going to personally be meeting all my potential matches for me?" is a great start. And if not, "Can I meet all the matchmakers on your team weighing in on my membership?" will help. "How large is your database?" is another useful question. There's currently no way of verifying the number, but gauging the matchmaker's response might be telling. I'd also want to know how many of my dates a matchmaker anticipates coming from their internal database as opposed to needing to recruit. Recruiting can be a common and worthwhile practice, especially when conducted in creative and thoughtful ways, but if a company employs this tactic, I'd want to know what their typical methods are. Additionally, what happens if you have a dealbreaker or two outside the ones listed in their contract? (For instance: *"I'm vegan and won't date someone who eats meat: I'm morally opposed to it."* I would want to know, ahead of time, if I were sent on a date with a meat-eater and we didn't hit it off, would my matchmaker still count that as one of my guaranteed introductions?) While they might assure you they'll do their best to accommodate your preferences, I would also get this response in writing.

I'd avoid asking about success rates, because everyone defines "success" differently, and without a governing body to fact-check it, the statistic simply becomes another sales tactic. One company I know claims an 80 percent success rate, which includes clients who get into relationships during their membership period regardless of whether they were introduced to their significant other through the service. They claim their "invaluable coaching" is what helped lead their client toward the right match, and take the credit. This might be true, but prospective clients usually assume the 80 percent refers to the matchmaking arm only. I'm always transparent with my clients if they inquire about success rates, and simply point to the actual number of clients my business partner and I have introduced to their spouses or significant others, voicing my hope to add them to that list.

When I first emerged on the scene, some competitors pushed back on my unorthodox business model, concerned it would threaten their bottom line. When their fears failed to materialize, and they realized they could benefit from indirect access to previously unknown singles through my extensive database, they wound up embracing me. Now I'm grateful to finally (and quite literally) have a seat at the table.

As I looked around at our group, I noticed that we'd unintentionally seated ourselves by generation: on one side of the table were the OG matchmakers with proven track records; on the other, the younger generation they'd helped mentor (and sometimes fear being replaced by). The former, possibly trying to keep up and stay relevant, had introduced a good deal of recent industry innovation. The newcomers, meanwhile, seemed more comfortable emulating tried-and-true business models and practices. I sat—both literally and metaphorically—in the middle.

"Is it my turn?" Barry had been waiting patiently for the floor. Attention shifted immediately his way—it always did, thanks to an appealing amalgamation of furrowed brow, earnestness, and a British accent. Though he was male, unmarried, and in his late sixties (a rare combination for a dating coach), he had found success in the industry publishing a book, hosting podcasts, and building a reputation as an expert in the "divine feminine polarity." After attending a seminar about how to take a more "masculine approach" to his dating life yielded enormously positive results for his own romantic interactions, he'd decided to forge a new career path and share his findings with the world. What consistently impressed me most, though, was his calmness. Other men in matchmaking tended to be more boisterous and hard-lined in their delivery. (I thought of Jimmy, a colleague who was noticeably absent today. A six-foot-four entrepreneur and former host of a reality show, he'd learned the matchmaking trade from his Chicago-based mother, and he once playfully insisted to me that no matchmaker was in it "purely for the love." I'd admired his self-awareness and ability to entertain, but sensed a whiff of projection.)

When Barry was done introducing himself, a side conversation brought up the difficulties of finding more masculine men in Los Angeles—a prevailing theory was that the California variety exuded "bisexual" energy. I hadn't been listening closely, but Melody put me on the spot: did I agree with her?

"Well, the lines are more fluid these days," I acknowledged. "For some. But I'm not sure lacking alpha energy, or possessing emotional openness, actually makes men 'bi.'" While her conclusion was a bit misguided, I could see how she'd arrived at it: many men moved to LA to pursue creative or arts-adjacent professions, and often those personalities were not the same ones who were especially outdoorsy or spearheading fantasy football leagues—and it's harder, sometimes, to match them. I often work with high-powered female clients—studio executives, agents, and others—who make decisions all day and hope for a "man's man" who will take some of the action and planning off their shoulders at home. "*That was the problem in my last relationship*," they complain to me. "*I had to do everything.*"

Their objections aren't entirely unfounded. Numerous studies have shown an overall slow and constant decline in men's testosterone levels over the past several decades, indicating there is a possible biological reason for their perceived lack of assertiveness and physical competence. Evolutionary social psychologist Dr. Sarah Hill has pointed to the male body's reaction to women on prolonged birth control pills—known to suppress women's estrogen levels. Others have speculated a rise in more sedentary lifestyles is a factor, or an increase of men in caregiving roles with more women in the workforce. Academic, author, and podcast host Scott Galloway explains that men these days are provided fewer opportunities to "demonstrate excellence."

I mentioned this to the group, and many of my colleagues nodded in understanding. Barry agreed something needed to be done.

"It's important for men to chase," he said, "and for women to choose."

Molly, a confident lifestyle influencer with deliberately dyed gray hair, let out a polite but noticeable scoff from the other end of the table. She specialized in setting up singles in nontraditional communities, from sex workers to those who participated in ethical nonmonogamy. (Rumor had it that she was a former adult film star and started her own business after another matchmaking company rejected her as a potential client.) I understood her reaction. After all, she had started her firm in pointed defiance of "the rules," and had no interest in engaging with them. Once again, I was somewhere in the middle. While I can see some merit in traditional gender dynamics, if I didn't allow for the gray area, I never would have asked out my husband!

Sometimes, I guess, rules are meant to be broken.

THE MEET-CUTE

When searching for your fairy-tale ending, *how* you meet your forever partner is far less important than meeting them at all. That said, I'll always be grateful for the fun, romantic, and original way in which I met mine—and I never saw it coming. I first met Dave in 2016 after his former employee Liz, a vivacious southern belle and *Tough Love* reality star, and my soon-to-be business partner Lauren conspired to get him to join our database (the hardest ten-dollar referral fee she ever earned, Lauren later told me).

At the time, I was in a toxic relationship I would take years to leave, but that didn't stop me from fantasizing what my dream man would be like. In my mind, he was over six feet tall, scruffy with a dark complexion, had impeccable grammar, and could easily be mistaken for Adrian Grenier. (Okay, fine, he *was* Adrian Grenier.) An almost five-foot-nine baby face who knew all the words to Biz Markie's "Just a Friend" was nowhere on my radar.

While Dave took my matchmaking process seriously, his approach to it was a playful one. Unlike the formulaic questionnaire responses I'd come to expect from others, his exuded personality. (When asked his age, he wrote: *"I'm thirty-seven, but most people think I'm younger. I'm not saying that to brag. I just have a youthful glow and spirit."* As for his ethnicity? *"White with a lot of flavor."*)

This shouldn't have been surprising, given Dave was an unscripted TV producer who earned his stripes working on shows like *Flavor of Love* and *Charm School.* He also wore loud clothes, pronounced words such as "water" and "daughter" with a heavy New York accent, and was secure enough in his masculinity to admit that Ryan Reynolds was "nice to look at." He was the perfect blend of charismatic and neurotic. When I first met him at the now defunct La Dijonaise Café in Culver City, I thought: *Wow. If I ever get the courage to leave my unhealthy relationship, this is exactly the kind of man I'd like to date.*

While Lauren helped convince him to give matchmaking a try, she flagged his possible immaturity. "He'll be tricky," she warned me. When I later asked Dave what he was looking for in a partner, I realized she might be right. Additional probing revealed that he thought there was nothing more attractive than "a woman with a little attitude who puts me in my place—while being cute about it." He also liked bachelorettes who "enjoyed a few cocktails from time to time," and who would likely be good company at Coachella. (*You know, the major priorities in life*, I thought sarcastically.) He also preferred someone not Jewish, convinced a Jewish woman would remind him too much of his own Jewish mother, sister, and cousins (a flattering comparison now that I know them all!).

"Since your pool's so big, maybe you can find someone Mexican or Latina for me?" he asked with a somewhat mortifying lack of filter. "I dated a local I really liked while shooting *I Love Money* in Mexico. But she lived far away, and her English wasn't great."

This guy is all over the place, it seemed. While normally that might have been cause for concern, his energy was positive, and he seemed relatively grounded. I chalked most of it up to humor. We set him up quite a few times, including with the creator of a popular NBC sitcom, but he wasn't connecting with any of his matches.

"*I think I prefer sweet and happy to sassy*," he relayed in a feedback email following another one of his humdrum dates. "*Just not too much of a goody-goody or run-of-the-mill 'nice.' I tend to reflect the energy of people around me, and I think if someone's too sassy, we'd just be playing a verbal game of chess and would occasionally actually hurt each other's feelings. Tomorrow I might feel differently about that*," he added.

His pattern of dissatisfaction was a red flag. He hadn't had a relationship last more than three or four months in nearly twenty years. Did he get annoyed too easily? Run at the first sign of imperfection? Or had he just not met the right person yet? He'd recently purchased a condo, supposedly with the intention of starting a family, but his seeming inability to commit was definitely worth considering.

Part of me hoped I could introduce him to a woman who would be the one to break that pattern, but then, out of the blue, he put his membership on hold. "*To be completely honest*," he wrote, "*I'm going on a fourth date tonight with a girl I'm starting to really dig*." His update should have thrilled me—he was putting himself out there and connecting with someone!—but I couldn't summon as much enthusiasm as I normally would in that situation. Why wasn't I happy for him?

I managed to respond: *"Fourth date is big! That's exciting!"*—accompanied by a lame smiley face emoji.

Figuring I might never hear from him again, I brushed off the exchange, but two weeks later, he resurfaced. "*The fourth date went well with her*," he shared with me, "*but the fifth did not. That's when we realized we had nothing in common. She was very quiet and pissy after I planned a nice date to watch* Fast Times *in the cemetery. I think she's more of a* Breakfast at Tiffany's *kind of girl. But I like that movie too . . . well, that's one thing we've got.*"

I chuckled at his reference to the Deep Blue Something song before I could stop myself. Why did I care so much about his availability? It's not like I could date him anyway. I was in a relationship. Still, Dave's existence proved to me there were other attractive, witty men out there. *For my clients*, I had to remind myself.

Over time, our emailing became more frequent, and I couldn't help but notice the slight pick-me-up I'd feel whenever his messages hit my inbox.

"*I've got a date tonight with someone my aunt fixed me up with*," he wrote in one unsolicited update. *"And some sweet action happening on* The League."

A week later, I asked whether his aunt was a better matchmaker than I was. "*People are so weird these days*," he replied. (I could practically feel his scowl through the internet.) *"That girl I told you about is also from New York, and just moved here in January. I hate how you can go on two great dates these days and then one wrong thing can be said over text or something and ruin it all. I'm never texting anyone again. I'm trading in my smartphone and getting a beeper."*

Our chats continued, and before long it seemed like we'd

touched on everything from his celebrity crushes to his ending his last "relationship" after the woman claimed Garfunkel was as talented as Simon. I told myself the conversations were strictly professional—we mostly talked about his love life, so I could help him get better results—but at a point, it became clear that his level of detail and disclosure was unique. My other clients weren't as honest or vulnerable with me, particularly about their concerns, or the more challenging parts of the dating process. So what did it mean?

"I think I'm gonna submit myself to being a lifelong ladies' man and am no longer trying to explore deeper romantic connections," he confessed at one point. *"Life is better with that mind frame."*

Ultimately, I made a hard but necessary decision. Knowing there were guys out there like Dave who posted silly thoughts on social media about watching *Dirty Dancing* on a rainy day, and who were adventurous enough to try eating a rat in Cambodia, was exactly the push I needed to finally break up with my ex. Some people would have taken their time after their relationship ended, perhaps to work on themselves, before pursuing something new. But I'd already done some of that development before, and had been mourning the failures of my last relationship mainly while I was in it. I finally reached a point where I knew what I deserved and, most important, felt ready to receive it. Maybe Dave was my person, or maybe he wasn't, but the only way to know was to try dating him.

The problem was that Dave had no idea I was single. As a matchmaker, I wasn't exactly advertising this recent change in relationship status. I did, however, have an inkling he'd be open to getting to know me better, as he hinted once I was his type. *"I swear, I'm not super super picky when it comes to looks,"* he shared, after growing self-concious about all the matches he was rejecting. *"I just want someone cute. For example, I think you are cute. (I'm not flirting with you or saying you are an example of how I'm not super picky because you aren't that cute.) I'm just saying . . . I don't know what I'm saying. I mean, you get it."*

Still, I had no technical confirmation he'd be interested in an actual date with me. But I was free for the first time in three years, and not feeling my usual fear of "putting myself out there." If I asked him out and he wasn't interested, the worst that could happen was that I'd lose him as a client. But he wasn't "having it" with any of our bachelorettes anyway. *To hell with it*, I figured. Even if he is a "three-to-four-month relationship" guy, I could stand to have three or four months of fun.

Before I stepped out of my comfort zone to test the waters, though, I ran the idea by Lauren. I teased that I might be interested in a date with one of our clients, and nervously wondered how she'd feel about that. She instantly lit up, saying she had confirmation he was into me too.

"Really?" I could feel myself getting excited.

"Yeah. He wondered what your deal was. Can I tell him you're single now, and he should just go for it?"

"Sure!" I couldn't believe my luck. "You're talking about Dave Kuba, right?"

"Dave Kuba?" She didn't even try to hide her surprise. "You're interested in *that* guy?" (She actually really liked Dave by then, but had already created a magical future in her mind where I was riding off into the sunset with this other mystery bachelor.) After some playful discussion, Lauren gave me her blessing. Out of habit, she also offered to reach out to Dave on my behalf, but I told her this wasn't middle school—I could handle it myself!

Dave had just returned from Coachella, and I emailed him, asking how it went. He shared he was finally "over it" and "ready for the next phase" of his life. "*But what does that mean?*" he wrote rhetorically.

"It means you should ask me out." I remember hitting the "send" button before I could overthink it. "*P.S.*," I added to try to keep things light. *"I'm aware of how unprofessional this email is."*

It felt like months before he eventually replied: *"I'm reporting you to the Better Business Bureau."* I panicked, but only for a moment. "*Just kidding*," he added playfully. *"Send me your phone number."*

Our texting was as seamless as our email banter, but it wasn't long before Dave pointed out that our dynamic felt imbalanced. As someone who had set him up multiple times, I already knew so much about him. To even the playing field a bit, could he ask a few questions about me?

"*Sure*," I agreed. It was only fair.

He immediately copied and pasted my company's intake questionnaire.

THE FATAL FLAW

"It will happen when you least expect it." According to some experts (and likely your mom), the best way to attract a significant other is to forget about wanting one at all. Who needs matchmakers, dating apps, or putting yourself out there when love is supposed to happen on its own?

Dave and I had been given similar advice on our journey to parenthood, as if ignoring his low sperm count (which he attributes to too much weed and Mountain Dew in college) would somehow be what wound up fixing it. The trite advice seemed to undermine the use of any kind of intervention, from vitamin supplements to IVF, which felt flawed, but accepting that some things are simply out of our control can be freeing. Leaving our fate to the universe allows us to go about our lives in a lighter fashion, unencumbered by self-blame. So, what is the right balance?

I mulled that over one morning as I prepared to contact Callie about her first official match, Jake. He was a friend's cousin whom I'd met a month earlier at a birthday party. While Jake didn't initially take me up on my suggestion to join my database, he was receptive when I reached out, specifically about Callie. The option of meeting a beautiful and accomplished woman not currently on the dating apps was too tempting to ignore. We did a quick Zoom soon after to confirm their compatibility, and by the end, I was convinced of it even more.

"*Meet Jake*," I wrote to her. *"He's 5'10", 43, and a witty, kind, and masculine SVP in the film industry."* Each time I emailed someone about a potential match, I personally tailored my description to appeal to them—no generic, one-size-fits-all blurb. The extra step was time-consuming for sure, but taking care to point out certain traits mentioned during someone's intake interview, or highlighting a mutual interest of theirs, can positively impact a client's attitude going into their date. It also makes them feel heard and respected in their search.

"*He's passionate about what he does for a living*," I continued. *"Has an appealing mix of nerdy and edgy qualities, and has a stable executive job while still possessing creative flair. He also loves dining out and live music like you do. I think you'll get along great! If you're down to grab drinks with him at Bacari, let me know when you're free."*

My suggestion for drinks was strategic. One trick I'd learned, when dealing with straight couples, was to always frame the date as "drinks" for the women, and "a light bite and drinks" for the men. If the bachelor wants to cut the date short, quick drinks is what the bachelorette was expecting. But if he throws in some appetizers, *he* thinks he's following directions, and *she* feels impressed. It sets them both up for success.

After sending his description to Callie, I leaned back a little in my chair, feeling satisfied. I'd already contacted a few other singles I'd been thinking of for her, but the act might have been superfluous if she wound up hitting it off with Jake. Because I don't promise a certain number of matches for clients, I'm able to encourage them to focus on one connection at a time, rather than being preoccupied by who's on deck.

Dating app culture has largely fed into the "next best thing" attitude, and I'm constantly searching for ways to counteract it. Rather than really getting to know someone who might be wonderful for us, swiping culture has created an illusion of choice. But "more" options doesn't always mean "better," and I fear that in the search for the "perfect" person, countless singles are overlooking the person perfect for them.

My next client, Meera, the one whose photos I was peddling at the matchmaking meetup, has the opposite problem—she isn't discerning enough. Despite her hopeless romanticism and near obsession with finding the One, she'd never really been in love, and it seemed like she was chasing an idea of it formed by watching 1950s Disney films like *Sleeping Beauty*. Every night that passed without being rescued by her prince felt like a waste of time to her.

I could hardly judge, as I grew up similarly influenced. I remember being single and believing that every unsuccessful first date or failed relationship was evidence I'd likely end up alone. Life had to be more exciting with a significant other, I reasoned—traveling, moving into a new apartment, getting a pet. What was the point of it all if I was doing it solo? I was metaphorically asleep, but if I met the right guy or had the right kiss, I'd suddenly wake up.

That mindset was unhealthy, though, and I was determined through coaching to help Meera reshape hers.

Name? Meera V****

Your age? 31

Height? 5'5"

Sexual orientation? Straight.

Where do you live, and what is your living situation? West Hollywood in a two-bedroom rental (love dogs but no time to take care of one yet).

Where are you from, and where else have you lived? San Bruno, CA; DC, for school; and did a semester abroad in Spain.

What's your profession? Film publicist for an independent film distributor.

Race or ethnicity? South Asian.

Religion? Hindu, but I'm not religious at all. I consider myself more spiritual than anything.

Your political views? Moderate. Not really into politics.

How important is it for you to marry someone of the same faith? Not at all.

What is your highest level of education? BA from Georgetown.

Most serious relationship and when/why did it end? I was with my ex for four years. It started off passionately, but by the end, we were more like best friends. I gained some weight during that time, and in the last year or so, he barely touched me. Can share more later.

Do you want and/or already have kids? No kids yet. I want four, and I think there's still time for that? If I meet the right guy soon.

Please describe your type, if you have one: Usually tall, pretty white boys. Ultimately, though, I just want someone people respect who is also humble, ambitious, and into family.

> **Do you have any dealbreakers?** No smoking or drugs, single dads, or anyone religious. I prefer someone who hasn't been married before either. And please, no receding hairlines.
> **Please list your hobbies:** Hiking, cooking, Pilates, farmers markets, exploring different neighborhoods in LA, bike riding on the beach, and watching anything on Bravo.
> **Tell me something about yourself not listed above. It's okay to brag:** I'm a part of a women's mentorship group that I'm really proud of. I love to travel. This past December I made it down to Antarctica, which means I only have one continent left to visit now: Australia. I understand Gujarati, and I hate dating apps.

"Hi, Jaydi!" Meera appeared on-screen surrounded by her usual blurred-out background. I wondered what people try to hide when they activate that feature: six cats? Dirty laundry? I typically find out sooner or later, either literally or metaphorically.

The attention on the foreground, though, allowed me to focus on Meera—most notably, her smile. Unlike the rest of her face, it was the only part that wasn't perfectly symmetrical, with the right corner turned up slightly more than the left. While this "flaw" felt more learned than biological, it somehow made her more beautiful and approachable at the same time. The only parts of her appearance not wholly natural were the dabs of pinkish-purple blush above her cheekbones that felt more arbitrary than deliberate. She looked happy today, which was a relief, and also a departure from more recent sessions.

I'd always connected and identified with her capacity for emotion, but we differed in the ways we responded to heartbreak. After any sort of devastation, I'd go into new experiences protecting my heart a bit more, determined to avoid making the same mistake twice. Meera, however, possessed (and embraced) the magnificent but also dangerous ability to forget any pain at all, and fall in love instantly with nearly every guy she ever dated. Everyone has some good in them, but sometimes that was *all* Meera saw in a person, ignoring other, more troublesome qualities—a detrimental tendency we'd spent a good deal of time unpacking together.

"So," I started, stating what I thought was the obvious. "Does this mean your date with Sal went well?"

Sal was a recent referral I flagged for her. An associate VP at a market research firm, he was creative, passionate, family oriented, and easy on the eyes, albeit a bit more gangly and with darker hair than Meera's usual "type." He also owned his place, was emotionally available, and even spent time in Australia, the top country on her bucket list. Introducing the two of them made sense, but I had wondered whether Meera was in a place yet where she could see Sal's full potential with her.

"He's a nice guy," Meera started, and my heart instantly sank. I could already tell the clichéd praise was more for my benefit than her own. "I just didn't feel sparks with him."

Ugh. I sighed. The S-word. It's not that I'm against sparks. I felt them when I first met Dave. But not all sparks are good—sometimes they light a tree on fire and burn down an entire forest. I looked again at Meera, trying to assess what was going on. And then, I saw it—an expression I'd come to know well: the mischievous grin of a client who knew she had "gotten away with" something.

"Okay, but you did feel sparks . . ." I guessed. "With someone else?"

Meera giggled, and I braced for impact.

"His name is Trevor, and he's a Capricorn. I've never dated a

Capricorn before," she added quickly. "If you can believe that." I nodded, trying to keep my expression impartial. I don't put a ton of stock into astrology, but Meera rarely goes on second dates without comparing birth charts first. "We met for coffee and kept talking. For five hours!"

"Wow," I allowed, recognizing the feat. "What did you two talk about for so long?"

"Everything! His divorce, his friends, his recent trip to Cabo," she gushed. "And he wants four kids, just like I do!" *Four*, I thought, slightly envious of her optimism. *At this rate I'll be lucky enough to have one.* "We're going on a third date on Sunday."

"A *third*?" I hoped she missed the crack in my voice. For some, a third date this soon would be promising. For Meera, it was potentially the beginning of a problematic pattern. She needed someone patient and committed to growing a relationship with her over time—not someone who led with passion and intensity but potentially lacked follow-through: the MO of her more recent situationships.

"He was at my place last night. But don't worry," she added quickly. "We didn't do anything. Just talked. All night."

She paused, waiting for me to jump in. I thought carefully before responding. Meera was rarely intimate with men she wasn't serious about, but once she was, she tended to get emotional if her deep feelings weren't immediately and fully reciprocated. She assured me that things hadn't become physical yet, but emotional intimacy—talking all night, multiple dates in rapid succession—could be just as powerful and dangerous.

I don't have rules or timelines for clients when it comes to sex, but I do try to help them prepare for all possibilities once it enters the equation. Whether or not two people will end up in a long-lasting relationship or eventually break up isn't determined by the act or the timing of it (my husband's good friend married a man she slept with on their first date), but sex usually provides clarity for those involved, and speeds up an eventual outcome. Walls tend to come down following it, and we often see sides of others we didn't glimpse beforehand. With the right person, this revelation can be life-changing. With the wrong match, it can lead to disappointment and hurt.

"And don't be mad, all right?" Meera launched into the climax of her story. I leaned in, trying to mask my concern. "He told me he loves me."

I thought about my twenties when I'd dated a coworker twelve and a half years my senior who started our relationship hot and heavy. His pursuit of me was both flattering and exhilarating, and after I reacted well to learning something he deemed shameful about his past, he told me he loved me. It was our third date. Our relationship had seemed promising—he was older, so telling me how he felt so quickly seemed like a sign of certainty and maturity. But as things progressed, his actions didn't align with his words. He enjoyed how I made him feel, but he made *me* feel uncertain and anxious. My gut told me I was a placeholder, that he'd taken previous objects of his affection to the same French restaurant and serenaded them with the same Billy Joel songs. (I would later learn I was right.) Rather than falling in and out of love easily, I speculated, he might never have felt it to begin with. A younger, less aware me would have stuck around, ignoring those concerns and relishing the scattered breadcrumbs thrown my way, but I had just come off a healthier two-year relationship and could tell that something about this new one was off. I didn't escape unscathed, but the damage could have been far worse if I hadn't had a more positive reference point.

I wanted to share all of this with Meera, but I could tell she was smitten, and it wasn't my job to lecture her based on my own history. "Is it possible," I wondered aloud, "that Trevor is simply a more open, sensitive kind of guy? The kind who feels emotions in a big way, very early on, and doesn't take the time to process them before sharing?"

"He said he's been waiting his whole life to find me," Meera said defensively. "You don't think that's true?"

I had to admire her idealism. I didn't doubt that Trevor had found in Meera a good person worth loving. She was. But I also knew her and suspected that on the date, she had been a captive and eager audience for whatever Trevor needed, leading him to overextend and her to overinterpret. When I asked whether their life perspectives and values aligned, she wasn't sure. Apparently, the hours of conversation they'd had together didn't scratch the surface of worldviews or religion. I asked how she'd feel if he attended church regularly, given that her family is Hindu. She said she'd be open, provided he'd celebrate their traditions too. The sentiment was great, but it was an untested one. I also wondered whether she had a sense of how he might handle conflict, and whether he knew about her tendency to keep things bottled up, afraid of scaring loved ones away if she expressed discontent.

There was still so much more to learn about each other, which was normal. But by receiving Trevor's declaration of love without protest, Meera was sending the message that she bought into his definition of it—which involved blind acceptance. A healthier form of love means accepting someone after really getting to know them, and feeling accepted by them in return—something that can only be earned over time.

Trevor's eagerness to drop the L-word so readily concerned me. Was this something he'd done before? Declaring feelings this early might feel like a welcome release to one person, but if shared before weighing its potential effects on the person you're saying it to, that can get messy. I've coached enough men and women prone to feeling more passionate emotions from the jump to not presume malicious intent; however, Trevor's toxic enthusiasm was the last thing Meera needed on her journey to find her husband. While that kind of energy might feel exciting to her, even more so would be the lasting connection she could make following a courtship of thoughtfulness and restraint. I also worried that if Trevor's affection were to become inconsistent, Meera might revert to spending months or years trying to make a relationship with him work rather than leaving herself open to other possibilities.

"Do you believe in twin flames?" she asked, as if our entire client-coach relationship depended on the answer. "Twin flames" is a niche dating term some mistakenly use interchangeably with "soulmates." Actress Megan Fox clarified the distinction on the podcast *Give Them Lala . . . with Randall*, sharing that a twin flame is "actually where a soul has ascended into a high enough level that it can be split into two different bodies at the same time. So we're actually two halves of the same soul, I think," she shared about her relationship with the musician Machine Gun Kelly. These types of bonds are usually more intense and volatile. There's even an alleged cult, Twin Flames Universe, that recruits new members based on the concept.

After weighing my response, I led by sharing my disdain for any theory that suggests a person can't be "complete" without another. I believe you can't find the right match for you without feeling complete first. "You also need physical chemistry to sustain a good relationship, an emotional and intellectual connection, similar life goals, a shared value system, trust, and healthy communication around conflict," I explained to her. "And you need time to make sure their actions align with their words. Anyone can talk a big game."

"You think that's what Trevor is doing?" Meera asked with a spike of worry in her voice.

"Not necessarily." The truth was, I couldn't possibly know Trevor well enough to understand his mindset. But my point was there was no harm in waiting.

I asked Meera whether she and Trevor were using labels yet. "Defining the relationship" is often one of the most difficult and overlooked parts of dating, especially in a world of apps and hookup culture. Many people slide into relationships without actively discussing them, or move forward without labels, worried that talking about it will cause the other person to bolt. It was entirely possible that Trevor saying "I love you" was his way of showing commitment and intention, but Meera admitted there was a lack of clarity there.

I tried masking my relief. This meant there was still time for Meera to slow down, but I had to navigate that conversation carefully. If I didn't seem supportive of her budding relationship with Trevor, she wouldn't feel comfortable confiding in me about him in the future. I also wanted to leave room for the possibility that he *was* everything Meera had been waiting for. Just because I was skeptical didn't mean I was right—plus, I could be harboring a bias, annoyed that she had so easily dismissed sweet Sal, my own recent choice for her.

I advised her to see how Trevor would treat her over time, but she was worried. "What if he wants to be boyfriend and girlfriend sooner?" If Trevor wanted to move faster, I assured her, it meant he really liked her, and wouldn't walk away just because she needed to move at a different pace.

"It's my job to help you consider all options, before you rule out the rest of the entire world as your dating pool," I told her. "Let him earn the right to be exclusive with you. You're worth it." I could tell from her familiar asymmetrical smile that the compliment landed. "If your connection with Trevor is as real and genuine as you say, he'll still feel this way about you in a few months from now. I promise."

She reluctantly agreed. Meera didn't need my permission or approval to escalate her relationship with Trevor, but I was glad, for her own sake, that she was seeking it out. To help assuage her anxiety about it, I suggested we set a deadline.

"If you both feel the same way two months from now, and Trevor's behavior is consistent, let's revisit the boyfriend conversation."

Meera nodded. Crisis averted, for now.

Drivers often slow down to ogle a car accident, a phenomenon called rubbernecking. The morbid behavior, which can lead to even more accidents, is both dangerous and ill-advised—yet it's human nature to observe, and to internalize what's in front of you in the service of self-protection. You watch the crash out of curiosity, but also because on some level, you want to know how it happened, and how to avoid it.

Dating is no different. We watch the people around us ruin relationships, and try to learn from them. Oftentimes, the most traumatic ones are the most educational. For me as a dating coach, rubbernecking isn't just an occupational hazard; it's a necessity. My job is to constantly study and learn from others' mistakes in hopes that examining one client's error will spare dozens more from the same fate.

As I thought about Meera, I wondered whether this was what having kids would feel like. How many times had my mother given me advice about a particular situation, only for me to dismiss it?

(If only we could trust objective and caring third parties the way we trust ourselves.) Many of us have to explore a potentially bad situation, though, sometimes multiple times, before we can recognize the consequences of it. The possibility of regret can make it feel impossible to walk away. *Sure, that might look like a red flag. But what if it's not? What if this time, with me, it's different?* We all have to learn the hard way, and for me, that took years. But once clarity came, it felt as if everything clicked all at once.

Rather than judge someone for not making what any reasonable outsider would deem the "right" choice—after all, many intelligent people make poor decisions, especially when it comes to finding love—it's my job to meet people where they're at, ask helpful questions, dole out productive advice, and comfort them all the same when they don't take it.

PRIDE AND PREJUDICE

A few weeks later, a "Save the Date" from a couple I helped match reminded me why I needed to remain focused on the end goal, even if some of my clients were taking more roundabout ways to get there. Getting invited to clients' weddings was a relatively new phenomenon. Out of respect for couples' privacy—particularly the more high-profile ones—I usually took a back seat after an introduction was made. But after several engagements and weddings took place without including me, I began to question if a more passive approach was best. I wanted to see the manifestations of my labor!

After years of missing out on this pleasure, I suggested to Lauren that maybe we could start triple-dating with some of our clients in an effort to get to know them as "units" rather than the individuals who initially signed up with us. The meetups that followed were fun, refreshing, and informative. We heard personal stories from them, witnessed looks of true love, and our very presence even nudged certain clients who weren't yet engaged to each other in that direction. By remaining in touch, we were also granted front-row seats to baby showers and other momentous life occasions.

"Shouldn't they be the ones taking *you* out?" my mother asked me one day. "To thank you?" She had a point, but I'm not one to sit around and wait for something I desire.

Something else I desired was to help form even more couples this year than I had in previous ones, and we were on track to do that—especially with the end of summer approaching. Singles who spent the last couple months living it up on vacation would typically return home to familiar feelings of loneliness that usually last through "cuffing season"—the colder time of year when daters are more likely to pair up. (A similar shift occurred following the COVID-19 lockdowns, which had made some otherwise independent singles realize how much they valued having a strong and supportive partner to share their emotional and physical space with. The opposite happened too. Nobody wanted to be "stuck" inside with the wrong person.)

Around this time, Kent reemerged to share that he was finally open to meeting Natasha, a bachelorette he'd passed on before due to her height. "*I'm 5'8" in heels*," he'd written to me earnestly, "*so I hope you'll make sure that Natasha's not just 'okay' with short kings, but seriously totes rad about this . . . Not looking for a woman who is walking in the door making concessions*." But after a month or so with uninspiring prospects, he reconsidered, and his feedback following their date was encouraging.

"*This was the most fun, comfortable, and friendly matchup so far*," he'd praised me. "*Tasha (that's what I'm calling her now) opened by saying something to the effect of, 'I already feel like we're gonna get along,' which could've meant that she immediately put me in the dastardly friend zone, or the emotional connection was so obvious and authentic that we were meant to meet. Because we had our hands on each other throughout the evening, and because we've texted numerous times since, I'm guessing it's the latter, but women are crazy. Let me know what she says. I had a great time."* Natasha, too, dropped me a line that she was excited about meeting Kent.

More good news followed. A small handful of our couples became official in July, and Anna, the woman who had referred Callie to us, sent along an update that her boyfriend, Marc, recently introduced her to his family. And even Meera, to my shock, was still dating the dark horse, Trevor. I was really curious to hear more about their relationship in our upcoming session.

The only major disappointment that summer seemed to be Callie. Despite her lofty goal of meeting her partner within the year, she hadn't allowed me to set her up *once*. The string of rejections had started with Jake, the bachelor I'd keenly described to her early on. She'd asked around about him based on the general description I gave, and discovered that her friend went out with him months prior—apparently an immediate disqualifier. She also shared she couldn't date anyone sober, which Jake was. This wasn't something we'd uncovered during our initial session together, so I tried not to read into it much. But she continued to reject others.

"I reread the details, and I'm wondering if it's Michael Smith?" she wrote to me about another bachelor's description. *"If so, his hairline kind of gives me the ick."* (I eventually learned she'd been Google-searching people using their phone numbers, so I learned ways to circumvent that.) When it came to Tom, she nixed him over the description of his salt-and-pepper hair, which she insisted was a "genetic" flaw not to be passed on to her children.

She'd alerted me she could be "picky" when we met, but I'd taken the warning with a grain of salt (-and-pepper hair)—after all, *everyone* should be discerning about whom they're going to spend the rest of their lives with. To me that isn't picky, it's smart. If a client brings a particular quality or trait to the table and expects the same of their partner, I'm always supportive of that request. For example, if a woman is really successful, she might want to hold out for a man as accomplished as she is. Or, if a man is in the top one percent of Bumble profiles, he might insist on only dating women with model-esque features. I don't believe couples need to be equals in every category, though—I've seen plenty of blissfully happy couples who balance each other out in different ways—but I'll never fault someone for trying to find that.

Singles I *actually* consider "picky" typically fall into one of two categories: insecure or delusional. When someone's insecure, they often worry too much about how others might perceive their partner, which can compromise the integrity of what they're searching for. For example, a former client of mine had remained in an emotionally abusive relationship because, to the outside world, her boyfriend appeared to be a "catch." Others might select a partner who will make them feel better about their own physical or emotional hang-ups. For instance, when a woman of size tells herself that only taller or broader men can make her feel safe and secure, that's because she needs someone by her side who will make her feel smaller and more beautiful. Similarly, if a man insists on finding someone significantly younger, he might be trying to forget his own insecurities surrounding aging. Wanting a partner who has qualities others envy is understandable, but only when those qualities are in support of what brings you joy.

Delusional daters, on the other hand, aren't looking for a partner on their level. They're looking to date "up," without realizing they're doing so. This inflated sense of self often manifests as an unrealistic view of whom they can attract. (How many people do we know who had one drunken make-out session in college with someone "out of their league," and now believe anyone less traditionally attractive is "beneath" them?) Attempting to "level up" through dating isn't new—Gen Z even has a term for it, "throning"—but this is usually a deliberate act driven by self-awareness.

I want nothing more than for a client to be enthusiastic about someone I introduce them to, but if they aren't embodying the type of match they want to attract, there can be a fine line between handing someone their "dream" person and setting them up for failure. Then again, sometimes that's necessary. As Maria Avgitidis wrote in her book, *Ask a Matchmaker*, it can be useful for a client's journey to "balance [their] wish list with a reality check." I once had a client talk a big game, but when I finally put a woman he deemed "hot" in front of him, he had trouble making eye contact with her and talked her ear off the whole time about creative ways to earn airline miles. Her dismissal was humbling for him, and provided me with an opening to talk about which women were actively looking for him back. Those women weren't "worse," I explained. They were actually better suited for him, and it takes a confident person to recognize the value in that. Once he began seeing himself through the eyes of his future partner, rather than women who weren't interested in dating him, and viewing that as *their* loss, he was able to date more intentionally, and experienced stronger connections as a result.

Callie didn't seem insecure or delusional to me, but some of the reasons she'd ruled out matches had nothing to do with whether they'd be compatible with her—some were even issues with solutions as simple as a new haircut. So, what was holding her back?

She'd also been traveling on and off ever since our initial session—for work mostly, but still a hindrance. While I'm all for clients living their best life, traveling that often is a common momentum killer in the beginning stages of any relationship—or, in Callie's case, a roadblock to starting one altogether. I really wanted to help her, but it was becoming clear that she was getting in her own way. And, as we both knew, time was of the essence.

It was starting to look less and less likely that I'd be getting a wedding invitation from Callie anytime soon.

I wondered whether I would ever get an invitation like that from Meera. I certainly hoped so, but at the pace she was going, I figured it might be a long time in the making. Despite their passionate start, Trevor hadn't said "I love you" since their second date, and he'd scaled back to seeing Meera only once a week (albeit for a consecutive two-day stretch over the weekend; these overnight visits almost always included some form of intimacy, but communication between dates was sparse).

As my Zoom with her started, I adjusted my settings so she could screen-share photos of them together. A striking six-foot-three with blue eyes and a full head of blonde hair, Trevor looked, I had to admit, every bit the part of Meera's ideal "Prince Charming." Their infrequent but intense encounters also seemed to be well documented, ranging from their selfies taken at Temescal Canyon to what appeared to be Trevor's kitchen.

"These are great," I told her, meaning it. "Have either of you posted these on your socials yet?"

"We're both pretty private," she replied emphatically, though I could sense the disappointment in her response. I'm not one to push social media, but knew nothing would have given Meera greater pleasure than the chance to publicly show off her newfound love interest.

She seemed to still be taking Trevor's lead on pace, which wasn't surprising given her dating history. For four years, she'd been in a relationship with someone who didn't make her feel desired. Their sex life was minimal, and it had taken a toll on her. I could see that Trevor was making her feel desired and happy now, and to her, that felt like progress.

"I just want to make sure he's not hiding you," I told her, my protective instincts kicking in. "It's still early, but we said we'd revisit the exclusivity conversation after two months. How are you feeling about that now?"

She looked baffled by the very question we'd spent the entire previous session deliberating.

"Who cares?" She scowled dismissively.

"Well, *you* did," I reminded her. I wanted her to recognize how Trevor's words weren't exactly aligning with his actions—less to prove I was right, and more so to better prepare her for a possible negative outcome. (In most areas of my life, I enjoy being right, but in my line of work, that often means heartbreak for someone I care about.)

"Do you think I should bring it up to him?" She frowned. "I know he's not seeing anyone else."

A series of cynical thoughts flashed through my mind: *If Trevor isn't seeing Meera during the week, and his communication is poor in between their dates, he certainly has time to date other women. And if this is happening, has he told them he loves them too? Or is he only seeing Meera, but made false promises earlier in one short-lived moment of intensity?*

The continued absence of stated exclusivity worked in her favor.

It meant I still had some wiggle room to convince her to see other people—and in the meantime, I could continue working on building up her confidence. She'd grown in that area since we first started working together, but I wanted her to get to the place where she wasn't afraid to voice her desires in a relationship, knowing that doing so would attract the *right* man rather than scare him away.

In addition, she was also on a journey in terms of how she viewed her body. Meera was a healthy weight, with some natural curves that she was constantly and unfairly comparing to the influencers populating her social media feed. I knew that embracing the body she was in would only increase her chances of finding everlasting love, because by loving herself, she would set her own bar for how she wanted to be treated. I'd instructed her to look at herself on her Zoom screen during an earlier session.

"This is who your future husband can't wait to meet," I reassured her. "I want you to look at her, and tell me everything you love most about what you see. What are her best qualities?"

Meera had thought about it, then listed her smarts, resilience, easygoing nature, and kindness. I'd waited for more attributes to follow, but they never came.

"I love all that, Meera," I remember sharing patiently. "But you can't see any of that in your reflection. What do you *see*?" It's not that I want clients to be superficial, but I wouldn't be doing my job if I pretended that physical chemistry, and carrying yourself with confidence, didn't matter.

"Are you not seeing your beautiful brown eyes?" The corners of Meera's lips turned up slightly. "Come on, I know there's more."

After some pushing, I'd discovered that Meera also loved her smile, as well as her legs. She'd acknowledged that she displayed noticeably more confidence when they were accentuated. As a small tip,

I'd advised her to start showing up fashionably late to dates, so that this asset of hers wouldn't be hidden under a table when first meeting someone. She mentioned she'd worn a cute tee with high-waisted leggings for her first date with Trevor, which was a victory considering where we'd started.

She had a long ways to go in terms of confidence, but there was only so much I could touch on. Attempting to offer guidance in areas outside my jurisdiction is a gray area, which is why I encourage many clients to supplement their journey to find outer love by using a therapist to help make progress with their inner love. But sometimes, it's a tough line to straddle. Over the years, I've had to develop a sense for when things are moving outside my usual territory. I ultimately concluded that if I can stick to the present in conversations, I'm equipped to handle them. ("I feel like my insecurities make me a bad flirt. Can you give me some pointers?" *Yes.* Versus: "I feel like my insecurities stem from a childhood wrought with physical and emotional abuse. Can you give me some pointers?" *Probably, but better to run it through a therapist first.*) On the flip side, multiple therapists have referred clients to me, and some of my favorite clients are actually therapists themselves.

The overlap is blurry, but there will always be actionable steps I can provide clients that don't involve delving into their childhood trauma. Eliminating sources of negativity is one. In Meera's case, the devil on her shoulder took the form of social media. When she scrolled through posts showcasing others' "perfect" bodies or partners, she felt as if she could never measure up. The relationship piece affected her most of all. Photos and videos of happy couples had reminded her that, like her old pal Sleeping Beauty, she was stuck in time, while the rest of the world seemed to be moving on without her.

"Maybe some of your friends are in the *wrong* relationships, and you're actually 'ahead' because you're taking the time to find the right person," I'd tried to reason with her. "Or, maybe life isn't a race at all."

I'd also brought up the Marie Kondo method, suggesting it could be applied to her digital world (the practice involves removing anything in your life that doesn't "spark joy"). She'd agreed, and started unfollowing Instagram feeds that had once triggered anxiety, paranoia, or sadness. I'd noticed a positive difference in her demeanor almost immediately.

Modeling for others how you wish to be treated is also crucial. Praising and speaking positively to the people you love is not only a nice thing to do, but it also invites others to respond in kind. Meera might initially question a "you look great too" from a friend, but after hearing it enough times, she might start to believe it. The line of thinking is similar to what some call "Lucky Girl Syndrome"—the idea that if you repeatedly declare how blessed you are, good fortune will follow.

"Okay, so should I break up with him?" Meera finally blurted. I hesitated to answer. Trevor had more red flags than a Canadian embassy, but if Meera wasn't able to identify them herself, she'd simply put up with more bad behavior in her next relationship.

"Let's save that question for our next session." Our time was almost up, and I made a mental note to talk to Meera about types of flags in dating. If I could get her to start differentiating between them, maybe she'd feel comfortable waving the white one soon with Trevor.

8

THE CONFLICT

Like building confidence and knowing how to flirt, recognizing red flags—or warning signs in a relationship that indicate potential problems—is a skill that can sometimes take time to build. Some red flags are easier to spot (such as some physical, verbal, and substance abuse), but others don't present themselves until after we feel comfortable in a relationship or, worse yet, have fallen in love. So early detection is key. I decided to frame my next session with Meera as a "general lesson" rather than focusing on Trevor specifically, as I figured that would make her less defensive and more receptive to the information (and better prepared for the future). I started by asking her what came to mind when she thought of red flags.

"I don't know," she answered reflexively. "Cheating?"

She started with what she believed to be a clear red flag, but in some ways, it wasn't. Did she mean someone cheating on her?

Or in their past relationship? If a person cheats on you, and early, that's not only a red flag, I would argue, but a reason to break up with them. Other scenarios, though, are more nuanced. If someone cheated in their past, disclosed it, and appeared to learn from their mistake, it might be more of a beige flag—a behavior or dating history that might give pause, but ultimately prove to be harmless.

Drawing a hard line at such a blatant betrayal might feel simple from the outside, and while I can't imagine forgiving my partner for the act, I try not to judge people who stay in relationships with someone who cheated on them. If the cheating happened years into a relationship, or there are children involved, I can understand the temptation to try and forgive the act—especially if it was only once, there was no emotional attachment at play, and the offending partner was remorseful afterward. While I've never experienced this myself, I've worked with enough clients who faced such devastating consequences over their transgressions that they're unlikely to repeat the behavior that resulted in them.

But what I imagined Meera was referring to, when she addressed possible red flags, is that someone's ability to betray a loved one in such a profound way can sometimes be a pattern. Cheating physically or emotionally can be a sign that they didn't have enough respect for that person to end their relationship before exploring something new.

"What if they cheated *with* you?" Meera wondered, which was a valid question.

"You might not picture them being able to do it to you, in that case," I replied, "but if they did it once before, they could do it again."

Meera nodded, taking notes.

Next, I moved on to problematic relations with friends or family. Some examples are codependency, withholding of approval, and broken connections. Codependency, or unhealthy mental, emotional, or physical reliance on someone else, is a major relationship killer. I once coached a stuntwoman who was involved with a man whose mom was still really attached to his ex. Inappropriately, the mom continued to spend time with her son's ex, even campaigning for them to get back together. Rather than put the kibosh on it, the man kept in touch with his ex to appease his mother. Until her boyfriend learned to exercise healthy familial boundaries, there would always be at least three people in their relationship.

While we're hesitant to admit it, we don't just marry someone else—we marry into their family. If it's a struggle for their family to accept a relationship with you, that's an unfortunate uphill battle, and perhaps one you might experience for a lifetime. If your friends or family are the ones reluctant to support your relationship, that's also worth considering. Are they being unfair, or is it possible they see red flags that you don't? We all have a knee-jerk reaction to defend the people we care about, so if your loved ones aren't the type to normally intervene, and are voicing concern now, that might be worth evaluating.

When it comes to people who aren't close with their families, I'm hesitant to label this as a red flag, because sometimes it's for understandable reasons (and they might be seeking to strengthen their bond with whatever family they create with their partner). But other times, their lack of closeness with a relative can be a reflection on *them*. Every story has more than one side: Don't simply buy into your partner's version because it's convenient. Express a healthy curiosity about broken family bonds, and without overstepping, try to get a sense of your partner's role in that. If they don't speak to someone in their family, could they cut you out just as easily one day? Do they believe absence is a valid way to solve conflict? Is this how they'll want you to handle conflict with your own family in the future?

This all seemed to resonate with Meera, so I continued onto the next red flag: inflexibility. The ability to compromise is essential in any healthy relationship, but some people are too rigid and set in their ways, hold too narrow a worldview, or refuse to waver from how they were raised—even if doing so doesn't bump against any of their core values. If you find yourself constantly bending to your partner's will while your own wants and needs are being disregarded, this is another cause for concern. Some older bachelors and bachelorettes, in particular, can be more stubborn and accustomed to routine. But, it's never too late to grow!

After, I tackled inconsistency, one of the hardest red flags to identify and accept, and one that's been studied in large-scale settings. In 1956, the psychologist B. F. Skinner conducted an experiment to evaluate the effects of intermittent reinforcement by rewarding rats with pellets when they pushed a button—only, for some rats, the pellets were dispensed *sometimes*, not automatically. Data found that the rats who were rewarded inconsistently actually wound up giving the most effort, and it turns out people behave similarly. When we're rewarded all the time, we tend to work less for it. The "hard-earned" prize, when doled out by, let's say, an emotionally unavailable partner, is often chased with more enthusiasm. To return to the "honeymoon" phase of a toxic cycle, we'll put up with practically anything to make that happen.

Finally, I was ready to cover intensity, a personal pet peeve, and the most pernicious of all red flags, because it often masquerades as a desirable trait in a partner. Intensity covers a wide range of behaviors, and it was important for Meera to be aware of all its various manifestations so she could be on the lookout for them with Trevor, or anyone else in the future. Pace was one, and a complicated topic to navigate. Moving too quickly can be cause for concern in a relationship, but so is someone not wanting to commit. So, what is the right "speed limit"? This is where a good head on our shoulders, and a regular gut check, is important.

If someone says "I love you" on the first few dates, before they've really gotten to know you—and I don't just mean the best version of yourself—this is a red flag too. If you value yourself highly, you might feel—"Aha! Finally someone who recognizes my worth! I feel seen!" And if you don't value yourself *enough*, you might be thrilled about the external, and much-needed, validation. Some people call this initial and sudden expression of deep feeling "love bombing"—a manipulative dating tactic disguised as excessive flattery. The turn of phrase is clever, but like many quick-fix definitions that have emerged around dating, I find it to be dismissive. While some of these "emotional terrorists" have sinister agendas (the jury was still out on Trevor), I don't believe the majority of singles who commit such offenses behave this way on purpose. If they do, it would be easier for intelligent women such as Meera to identify.

It's possible I have a blind spot—I tend to empathize with my clients—but years of experience have led me to believe that most people are well-intentioned, and that any hurt inflicted on others is an unfortunate result of immaturity or unacknowledged pain. Often, men and women who spill the "L-word" too soon are bigger romantics than we are! The difference is that they presume love from the outset, when they're feeling a connection with someone, rather than waiting for it to grow over time. This often leads to their recipients not living up to the ideals they have built up in their heads, and the relationship winds up imploding. One day their declaration of love might translate to a more permanent feeling with someone, but encouraging them to take more time to be thoughtful about it, to conclude whether their feelings are temporary, will only prove beneficial in the long run.

"I think Trevor meant it with me," Meera insisted.

I didn't push back. "He probably did," I assured her gently. "Let's just call it red flag *territory*," I suggested. Questioning her implicit faith in this matter was important, because I wanted her to be more thoughtful when weighing exclusivity, and there was much to consider here.

I shared with her what I share with all clients. If you're really right for someone, and you've been dating less than three months, they'll be patient as you explore other options, provided you're receptive to them doing the same. If they're pressuring you too much otherwise, this is worrisome. While it's flattering to be pursued, once you've defined your relationship with them, you'll be more likely to overlook less desirable aspects of their personality that haven't emerged yet—so if your instincts are telling you to take more time before committing, then do it.

For those who normally rush in, I challenge them to wait a little longer. I'm often frustrated by my more "passionate" clients who—after meeting someone for a second at Miley Cyrus's birthday party—cancel on a meaningful introduction I have for them because they're convinced they just met their soulmate. Time and again, those same clients hit me up weeks later to share that it didn't work out with their potential partner (only to learn that the match I had in mind for them is no longer available). If they had slowed their roll a bit and waited to see if the connection was a lasting one, while keeping other options open in the meantime, they would have been better off. Determining when to become exclusive with someone should be based on a number of factors, but those factors shouldn't, and frankly can't, be determined after only a handful of interactions.

Moving too slowly, on the other hand, is just as alarming, and is sometimes tied to our attachment style. Attachment theory, which originated from the collaborative work of J. Bowlby and M. S. Ainsworth in the 1930s, helps explain why some people are reluctant to commit. Different attachment styles, or ways in which people behave in relationships (including their desire for closeness and intimacy) can be traced back to childhood and how our parents responded to our needs—the healthiest being a secure attachment. An anxious attachment style is another common one, typically marked by a higher need for reassurance.

But when it comes to dating, avoidants are who you want to, well, avoid. Having strict parents who encourage suppression of feelings, or having parents who are emotionally distant themselves, often results in kids with an "avoidant-dismissive" attachment style. These children might grow up to be strong and independent on the outside, but they typically struggle to make meaningful connections with others, and have a low tolerance for affection. Rarer is someone with a disorganized attachment style, known as a "fearful-avoidant" type. This develops when a child fears the one person who's supposed to be their source of safety, due to abuse or even inconsistency. In relationships with those people, the highs can be really high, but the lows can be even lower. I always encourage clients like Meera, who might be dating someone who fits this description, to ask themselves a couple of telling questions, such as: *Has this person made me cry recently? Am I holding back whole truths when discussing them with my friends?*

While I supposed Meera had told her close circle of friends about some of her anxieties surrounding Trevor, I bet she subconsciously softened the blow by embellishing his displays of affection and other positive signs he intended to move the relationship forward. In the early stages of dating, we often focus exclusively on a partner's more winning attributes, especially if they help mitigate the ones that cause us pain. Meera wasn't alone in dating someone with a potentially avoidant attachment style, as this type comprises approximately 27 percent of the population. But as time passes and people with other attachment styles wind up in healthy relationships, avoidants start comprising an even larger percentage of the dating pool.

Setting realistic deadlines when dating someone like this is helpful, but only if you stick to them. If you say that you're going to break up with someone if they won't commit to exclusivity after six months, then do it. If you say you're going to break up with them if you're not engaged after three years, then do that. The biggest mistake in dating someone with commitment issues is extending a deadline and giving them an even longer time to be indecisive. We think we're setting our relationship up for more success by giving our partner more time to process, but in reality, we're subconsciously sending the message that we're okay with their inaction. If you walk away, and they come after you, then great. If they don't, you've saved yourself additional time and heartache. It's important to note that deadlines should not be ultimatums issued to your partner, but more so, internal ones to hold yourself accountable. If you need to, share that deadline with a friend, and insist they hold you to it.

Attachment styles are deeply embedded in our personalities, requiring a great deal of therapy and dedication to help change them, so if you think you're dating someone avoidant, typically it's best to move on. As for the recommended "speed limit"? After three to six months of consistent dating, you should be on the same page in terms of exclusivity.

"When should you meet someone's family?" Meera wanted to know next. The answer was nuanced. Factors such as how often two people are seeing each other, or whether their family lives in town, needed to be taken into consideration. She wondered whether meeting them should be a precursor to exclusivity.

"No," I answered truthfully. "That step usually comes later. But if that person isn't ready to introduce you anytime soon, it's something you should evaluate."

Another form of intensity worth examining was controlling behavior. To help illustrate my point, I chose to share about my own, previous controlling relationship, so Meera could potentially learn from my experience—and know I wouldn't be judging her over Trevor. She looked surprised as I opened up, almost shocked someone like me could wind up in that situation. (Most people who've never experienced it don't understand how a strong, independent, and successful person could be so manipulated. But manipulation is gradual—just ask Anna Kendrick or Olivia Munn, who've both publicly claimed they survived relationships wrought with emotional abuse.) The problematic behaviors slowly seep in over such a long period of time, often counterbalanced by lavish gestures and false promises, that by the time you realize you're in a toxic relationship, you have to decide whether you want to cut ties with someone you've already developed deep feelings for—which is why recognizing early warning signs is important.

"So, what are they?" Meera asked, enraptured.

"Well, at the beginning, someone might only be telling you what to eat for dinner or what shows to watch." I studied Meera's face, searching for any sign of recognition, but I couldn't get a good enough read. "Depriving you of choice is how it starts," I continued. "Sometimes, though, it's even less direct."

My controlling ex would never blatantly tell me which friends and family to keep around, but he did criticize certain people in my life enough that it made me question whether I was a good judge of character. This boyfriend of mine was extremely intelligent, charming, and athletic, and best of all, he seemed crazy about me. Plus, when I finally worked up the courage to confront him about what certainly felt to me like his control issues, he *acknowledged* he had them (surely a good sign, right?), and said I was a perfect match for him because my strength and independence could "help keep [him] in check." In retrospect, I feel this was a classic manipulation tactic of making me believe our dynamic was exactly the kind he needed. But what kind of person did *I* need? And who was looking out for that? Many attempted breakups later, despite a significant run that seemed to be creeping toward an engagement, I couldn't shake the conviction that someone else was out there who could make me feel truly seen in a relationship.

Since starting my coaching business, I've not only worked with survivors of these types of relationships, but also coached some of the abusers themselves, which has been deeply insightful and cathartic. Some offenders are people used to "being in charge" at work (think attorneys, CEOs, directors, etc.); others lack control in other areas of their life and use their relationships as a way to gain it. Most people I work with who fit these descriptions don't see their behavior as problematic at first. Inflated self-worth and fragile egos often accompany these personalities, which makes their ability to recognize their bad behavior even trickier. This is why I typically only see real change in these clients after working with them for extended periods of time.

Gaslighting is another manipulation tactic you often find in controlling partners. Gaslighters convince you that your reality is untrue—something that ultimately undermines the relationship you have with yourself. By downplaying the harm they've caused you, or belittling you for questioning them about it, they might make you doubt your own instincts and memories. Eventually, they make you believe that you need them in order to make more sound decisions, and it's this dependency that makes it so hard to leave.

"This is a lot," I acknowledged to Meera. "We can go over any of it again later, if you have questions."

"I do," Meera responded. "But for now, should I be worried about Trevor? Or do you think I'm in an okay place with him?"

"Well," I answered honestly, "I'm mainly worried that you're not *calling* him your boyfriend yet, but you're acting like he is."

"Are you saying *I'm* a red flag, Jaydi?"

I couldn't help but laugh. "How about we save that question for another session?"

"Okay. But you might be surprised," she shared, knowing full well she'd catch me off guard, "that I'm talking to someone else on Bumble."

"You're on Bumble?!" Once again, Meera dropped a major headline far too casually. "When did this happen?"

"Well, I never technically went off it. I just wasn't using it for a while. His name is Raj," she added, amused by my predictably stunned reaction.

"Raj? As in . . . ?"

"Yes. He's also Indian," she confirmed. Ever since I'd met Meera, her parents had been pressing her to date guys from a similar background, but like my husband and some other clients who hail from other minority groups, she'd always insisted they reminded her of family. Apparently Raj was first-generation American and didn't usually date other South Asians either. Through the app, the two had discussed their mutual desire to have kids and attend an upcoming Nick Cave concert together. The length of the back-and-forth conversation was a little more than I usually recommend prior to a first meetup (I'm a fan of cutting to the chase and seeing whether there's any in-person chemistry sooner rather than later), but I was excited that Meera was still leaving room for other possibilities. Perhaps we were making progress after all!

At least I thought we were, until she said: "I do feel like I'd be cheating on Trevor if I met him, though."

I understood the sentiment, but encouraged Meera not to feel guilty about it. Until Trevor was willing and proud to call himself her "boyfriend," she had every right to accept dates from others.

"You always said actions are more important than words, though, right?" Meera challenged. I had said that, but her usage was an oversimplification. The ideal relationship offers multiple forms of validation, which Trevor wasn't currently giving her.

"You might be right about him," I appealed to her hopefulness. "But until he's ready to discuss exclusivity, if that's even still what you want when it happens, you should remain open to other options."

She promised she'd consider it, then asked whether I could approve her outfit for her date with Trevor that night. I nodded; I would always jump at the opportunity to remind Meera how beautiful she was. After disappearing from the screen for a few moments, she emerged in a cute sweater and light-colored jeans. I could tell she felt good in the outfit, and confirmed the combo was the right call.

Whether continuing to date Trevor was the right call was ultimately for Meera to decide.

ACT TWO

HERE'S LOOKING AT YOU, KID

Kent was troubled by the away message in my email. "*You can't just disappear on me*," he responded obstinately. I leaned back into my pillows and groaned. I'd been recovering from a polyp removal surgery—necessary to prep me for an additional round of IVF—but it seemed Kent interpreted my need for self-care as a personal affront. Natasha, the taller bachelorette he'd been excited about, canceled on him last-minute before what would have been their third date, and he was insistent on processing her "rudeness" with me.

While I normally would have stood my ground—or in this case, my bed—I agreed to hop on the phone with him later that day to talk through it. The gesture wasn't entirely selfless. I was, truly, curious what he'd say. I had some insight from Natasha, who'd emailed me as well, hoping to explain "her side."

Supposedly, on their second date, Kent spilled the tea on all his previous matches and his exes—including the mother of his two kids. (I'd already lectured him about discussing other relationships this early, but apparently the advice didn't stick.) He not only dominated the entire conversation, regaling her with work tales in an effort to impress her, and opened up about his relationship with his father in an effort to appear more vulnerable, but to my exasperation, he also dropped the "L-bomb" in an effort to . . . well, express love. At first, Natasha had been flattered. But after processing the bizarre experience with several of her girlfriends, she came to the shrewd conclusion that Kent's declaration had had nothing to do with her. He barely knew her. So rather than accept his Tom Cruise moment as a precursor to marriage, she saw it for what it was: a red flag. *Wow*, I thought. *Maybe she could have a word with my girl Meera.*

"Are you okay?" Kent greeted me. "You don't sound too good."

"I'm fine," I replied curtly. I considered telling him about the tests doctors were running to find out the receptiveness of my uterus, but thought better of it.

He quickly moved on to his favorite subject: himself. He monologued about everything—challenges with his latest movie, California's harvest season—everything except his date. I smiled politely as he hammered on about his nightly ritual of picking grapes (apparently, wineries like his usually harvested between midnight and early morning due to the cooler temperatures, which helps stabilize sugar levels and maintain the fresh fruit aromas—who knew?) and asked where I lived so he could send me a bottle of his latest Chardonnay, an offer I appreciated but respectfully declined. I didn't anticipate Kent showing up on my doorstep anytime soon, but preferred to keep the details of my home life private, including my address. (Lauren, however, would have had no qualms accepting the gift. "He could find me on Zillow anyway," she'd say. Plus, her nine months of forced sobriety were now over. "Bring it on!")

By the time our conversation finally got around to Natasha, Kent had worked himself up to detail everything wrong with her, along with the fickle nature of women in general. And then, before I could challenge his troublesome core beliefs and offer him some guidance on his impulsive tendencies, he said he had to run.

"I've decided to take a break from matchmaking," he declared, almost as an afterthought.

Wasn't he the one who was just annoyed about me *disappearing?* I sat up quickly, only to feel a sudden pain run through me. This is what I interrupted my recovery for?

I knew by now that clients request dating breaks for a variety of reasons: travel, work schedules, or even insecurities—like the prior winter when Meera was "feeling fat" and wanted to wait until she'd lost a little weight so she could feel more confident. (I tried talking her out of it anyway. She could work toward dropping the weight if that's what she wanted, but there was no reason not to meet men during that process.)

But Kent wasn't worried about his body; he was worried about his ego. He could have chosen to feel excited that as a team, we were finally tapping into more of what he was looking for. Instead, he went into self-preservation mode and removed himself from the dating pool entirely.

"So, you're saying if I meet another woman you might like," I clarified, "I shouldn't tell you about her?"

"I'm not saying that," he started to backtrack. "I'm saying only reach out to me if you have someone spectacular. Okay?"

That's the only time I ever reach out to you, you nitwit, I thought. But I was cordial and ended the call politely. As I ran through everything I knew about Kent's history, I realized it wasn't much. In addition to revealing little about his upbringing or family, he'd been actively avoiding the subject of his prior dating life, which meant I didn't have many clues as to how he felt about love, commitment, transition, or, importantly, rejection. Anything I'd been able to piece together had been from offhand comments made during more conversational parts of our sessions. (For instance, I knew Kent's relationship with his ex-wife only became copacetic after she remarried and no longer required child support—something he'd shared while flippantly referencing her "new family's" vacation to Ibiza.) But had he ever been in love with her? Had he ever felt love with *anyone*? Or was the best for Kent yet to come? I truly had no idea.

What I did know was that if he kept up this "tough guy" act, he was never going to wind up happy. He was in touch with his feelings, but perhaps not the right ones at the right time. The disparaging way he'd discussed Natasha meant he wasn't in love with her (no shock there), and my instincts and experience told me that based on his ability to conveniently dismiss his passionate declaration on their date and sail into anger, this wasn't the first time he'd behaved this way.

I sympathized with Kent. He felt emotions in a big way. A person doesn't "threaten" their matchmaker with a dating break otherwise. But it was important for him to consider how others might process his big feelings before sharing them so willingly. It's selfish not to, and I knew he could do better.

I crawled back into bed later that night and, despite my better judgment, began crafting an email to Kent. I wished him luck on his solo adventure, and threw in some tips and tricks in the hopes that—should he meet a fantastic woman in my absence—he wouldn't blow it by being too intense or talking too much. My pointers would probably fall on deaf ears (he wasn't exactly known for his listening skills), but at least I'd have tried every possible way to get through to him, even if it was no longer my job. I felt like an eager employee wanting to leave a good impression on my boss even though I'd just been fired.

I turned my computer off and put my phone on silent, sitting in the dark with Dave, who was already asleep beside me. Kent's session today had been a good distraction from my discomfort, but I was mentally drained. Investing so much time and energy in a client only to have them disappear—temporarily or forever—was always tough, and it could leave a scar if he ever circled back. The threat of someone checking out is enough to cause mistrust in any relationship.

I knew this firsthand from Dave, and thought about the early months of our own relationship when a similar threat felt palpable. "I think it's romantic for couples to break up and then reconnect in the future," he'd once told me. "Don't you think?"

I did not think. I fought a growing pit in my stomach. "Romantic is knowing someone will always be there for you," I protested. "How am I supposed to keep dating you now, knowing that you're probably going to break up with me at some point just because you think it's *romantic*?"

"Relax." He grinned, not realizing how seriously I was interpreting what he thought was a cavalier comment. "You have nothing to worry about. I was talking hypothetically." I appreciated the course correction, but the damage had been done. I spent months afterward slightly on edge, worried about getting too close to him in fear he was going to leave me. I knew that he'd already sort of ghosted the woman he dated right before me. The two had spent a decent amount of time together, and while never exclusive, he cut things off with her, seemingly out of the blue. (He did send a message to say he wouldn't be seeing her anymore, but no explanation as to why.) When I'd found out about her existence later, I was shocked. My usually thoughtful and kindhearted boyfriend had essentially disappeared on someone?

"What was I gonna tell her?" he inquired innocently. "That I met someone else better?"

"Not *better*, Dave," I'd scolded him. "Better for *you*. Wouldn't it have been more considerate to say that? To at least give her some form of closure?"

It's easy to write off ghosters as selfish, but it took that experience for me to realize that sometimes, they evaporate in an attempt to spare feelings. That doesn't make it okay, though. I believe that most women and men can handle the truth, and usually, they'll move on faster knowing it. Otherwise, they'll be stuck asking questions that wind up hurting themselves: *That person didn't even respect me enough to be straightforward—am I that easy to dismiss? Did our time together, however brief, mean nothing?* A parting conversation might be uncomfortable, but not having one can feel worse for the aggrieved party.

I thought about a popular influencer Alanna Noel, whose podcast I'd once appeared on. During our conversation, she mentioned how she made a regular habit of ghosting men without ever weighing the potential effects of it. "What if that guy meets someone amazing tomorrow, but he's in his head now thanks to your ghosting, and doesn't work up the nerve to approach her?" I challenged.

She was gutted. "I've never really thought of it that way."

Kent did warn me he was going to disappear, which was better than ghosting, I supposed, but if he were to return one day, I wondered how that would affect our relationship moving forward. At least in that instance, I'd be getting paid.

BUILDING CHARACTER

I closed my eyes in yoga class, trying to put the Kent business out of my mind. While it doesn't always seem this way to our clients, matchmakers have insecurities too. When a date goes wrong, when I peg someone incorrectly, or when a client vanishes, it's hard not to question my instincts. Despite the good handful of marriages, engagements, and babies I'd helped create, I started to wonder whether I really possessed the qualities needed to take my skills to the next level. Perceptiveness, humility, flexibility, empathy, and confidence were all essential to serving my clients best, but right now, I was questioning if I had the right balance of any of it.

Anyone can pick up on cues about someone's personality and preferences, but to be *perceptive*, a matchmaker has to detect less obvious traits and truths. For example, if a man says he's looking for someone "active," he might be referring to a partner's look more than their lifestyle. Or similarly, if he says "personality is more important," but then sends you photos of flawless-looking models he swipes right on, your first match for him better be a looker if you want him to "trust" you. Men often sugarcoat their preferences—especially the more superficial ones—to me and my business partner, believing that because we're women, we might get offended otherwise. They also tend to censor feedback following their dates if they detect the other person isn't interested in them back, self-conscious about showing their cards. If we couldn't read between the blurred lines, we'd be less effective at our jobs. Men aren't the only daters who aren't always candid, though. For example, if a woman says she's open to all socioeconomic classes but flies private and drives a Ferrari, she might be trying to avoid judgment and, in fact, prefers someone more financially comfortable. I'd always thought I was perceptive, but I also thought Kent and I had a good rapport—one that would make it difficult for him to so casually disappear on me. I was wrong.

Next I thought about humility. If you're a matchmaker or dating coach looking for credit every time you accurately make a prediction—positive or otherwise—you're in the wrong profession. I can recall several times I'd pitched a joke in TV writers' rooms that was glossed over, only for another writer to pitch an identical one moments later and for it to be well received. This used to infuriate me. But when it comes to helping people on their journeys to find love, you have to remove ego from the equation.

There's also humility involved in recognizing that, given the right personality and dedication to the craft, anyone can do what we do. While some claim to be "born" with the gift to connect people, most of what's needed to succeed in our profession is learned on the job. After all, predicting which singles will couple up well, for the rest of their lives, is a skill that can only be sharpened by failure and experience. As I listened to the singing bowls and soothing nature sounds on the class's soundtrack, I thought about clients who broke the mold—such as my unscripted producer client who shared her preference for "pocket-size men," or the data scientist who actively sought women with pronounced jawlines. I'd also predicted the outcome of many successful relationships, but had been surprised when certain singles didn't hit it off, and tried my best to learn from those interactions (such as an e-commerce CEO who only ordered water during our restaurant meetup, but wowed his dates following a little coaching).

Once I'd accepted that my instincts weren't always right, I adopted more flexibility in my practice. Even in cases where my intuition is correct, clients don't always follow my advice. In the beginning, I talked dozens of daters into going out with someone they weren't originally open to, and it rarely led to success. If they had a fixed notion of what package love would come in, I'd found it was best to try to deliver that first. After enough strikeouts, they'd hopefully come around and let me take a less predictable swing (e.g., how I was able to convince Kent to meet someone Natasha's height). Still, that hadn't been enough.

"Desire for a relationship is not the same as readiness," my colleague Carina—whom I ran into at the matchmakers' meetup—once wisely summarized the oft overlooked truth. Perhaps I was trying so hard to find Kent love that I hadn't stopped to question if he was ready for it. And maybe, just maybe, him taking a step back from dating was in his best interests after all.

Despite my attempts at remaining objective, I tend to get swept up in the emotion of it all. I suppose this is where empathy comes in—a skilled matchmaker's double-edged sword. By being able to see the world from clients' perspectives, I'm more easily able to identify with their journeys, understand them, and find suitable partners as a result. (I've watched some matchmakers operate who lack empathy, and these are often the same business owners guilty of treating clients like numbers moving through their "system.") But my empathy can sometimes cloud my ability to think objectively. I can also be a harsh self-critic. Nearly two decades into the job, I still haven't found a way to separate clients' joys and disappointments from my own.

Their failures, or lapses in judgment, are not my fault, I had to remind myself as I lay in savasana. For the last minute of class, I thought about the final characteristic of what I believe makes a good matchmaker: confidence—the category I was most wavering in today. The last time I remember feeling this way was when I initially contemplated the coaching side of the business. *Do I have enough knowledge and experience to fill multiple hour-long sessions with clients? Who am I to advise them on their dating lives when my own love life is in shambles?* Only after Dave and I began dating did I feel ready. It turns out my confidence didn't come from dating him, though—but rather from the faith in myself that I was able, finally, to put my own advice into practice.

If Kent were to resurface, I decided I would shelve the women I planned to introduce him to—a creative hairdresser, Cindy; an independently wealthy fitness instructor, Vanessa; and, most promising, an older and whip-smart financial advisor, Rita—until he made more of an effort to work on himself. And in the meantime, I had other clients to focus on who appreciated my help.

"Slowly, begin to wiggle your fingers and toes," the yogi before me commanded, offering a gentle transition out of corpse pose. "And when you're ready, please rise. Inhale your arms up over your head, and exhale them down to your heart, in prayer. And remember:

you are here to share, not to be perfect." He paused for a couple of breaths, and I smiled at the appropriateness of the mantra.

"Namaste."

As I prepped for a meeting with Lauren, I started to consider whether I was taking on too much. In addition to running to doctors' appointments, I'd been hired to write on a new animated series for Netflix, which meant I'd have to book clients and coaching sessions around a soon-to-be-rigorous writing schedule. Our matchmaking season was also ramping up significantly, with referrals flowing in due to pandemic-related relationship issues. (Bumble even coined the term "New Dawn Dater" for anyone who'd recently ended their long-term relationship.) The public's interest in our industry also piqued after the premiere of *Indian Matchmaking* on Netflix.

The show wasn't the first time matchmaking had captured the pop culture imagination. Patti Stanger had risen to fame through her show *Millionaire Matchmaker*, which followed her as she set up wealthy individuals searching for love; there was Darren Star's *Miss Match*, starring Alicia Silverstone, who had also played an amateur matchmaker as the lead in *Clueless*, an adaptation of Jane Austen's *Emma* (and a new iteration featuring Anya Taylor-Joy), and *Hello, Dolly!*. And lest we forget, of course, the classic theatrical production of *Fiddler on the Roof*, Sarah Michelle Gellar's character in *Cruel Intentions*, and the matchmaker Kelsey Grammer pines for in the last season of *Frasier*. Matchmaking was having a moment, and I was glad to be part of it.

I was also grateful Lauren was finally back from maternity leave. She could run point while I focused on my other commitments, but she had a bit of catching up to do, including meeting some newer clients of ours. They would be in great hands, but she agreed to keep me posted on any potential introductions before they happened.

As I glanced through our master list of clients, I provided recaps on where each stood on their journeys. For the ones in newly formed relationships, we planned to check in and see how they were doing. (I'd always hated to see a connection fall apart simply because one person forgot to stay in touch with another while on vacation.) We also decided to preemptively reach out to people we hadn't set up in a while with updates. Like agents who submit their clients' work for consideration often without their knowledge, Lauren and I do a ton of behind-the-scenes work for clients that they're unaware of. Updating them regularly would be a full-time job itself, but I try to touch base once or twice throughout their memberships to let them know we're thinking about them and to help maintain confidence.

Lauren asked if I followed a client of ours, Mariel, on social media. I didn't, so she excitedly shared with me that Mariel just posted her first public photo on Instagram with a guy we set her up with a while back, Kenji. "I think they're official now!" I leaned over to take a look. Lauren had always been great at keeping tabs on our clients—even former ones—online. I had to laugh at the entire world finding out about their hard launch the same time we did, but chances were they would drop us a personal note later that week.

I also wanted to fill Lauren in about recent setups: Heather, a celebrity assistant she and I matched previously, was now going on a second date with a dynamic and femme literary agent I'd sent her way. Similarly, a new client, Brandon, was going on his third date with Kate, the high-pitched hottie Kent had rejected. We also discussed two new bachelorettes I hadn't matched at all yet. When I activated the first's membership, I'd had several men in mind for her—but now one was unavailable due to a death in the family, and the other had recently become exclusive with someone else he met on his own. So I needed to regroup. The other bachelorette was also fantastic, but wildly different from the impression her intake questionnaire had given. After talking it through, Lauren and I landed where we always do: waiting for a new referral we were excited about rather than setting her up with a subpar option. *Quality over quantity*, we reminded ourselves.

Then, we shifted our conversation to more challenging clients like Callie. I'd sent several frustrated emails about her to Lauren since she signed up, and now Lauren wanted to know "how bad" Callie actually was. I shared that Callie was great, but like many others who came before her, she'd been getting in her own way. "These people I'm presenting to her are, objectively, amazing catches. Who knows—maybe you'll have better luck."

"I think you've been too nice," Lauren told me matter-of-factly. "You should give it to her straight."

Lauren wasn't wrong. I'd been stewing, growing more and more impatient with Callie's constant rejection of bachelors and bachelorettes since we started working together, but kept it all to myself. I'd been patient, trying to get to the bottom of why she wasn't receptive to any of my matches, but my patience wasn't helping her.

It was time to give her some tough love.

I WISH I KNEW HOW TO QUIT YOU

"If you're looking to be off the market in the next ten months, something needs to change," I started brusquely, already a bit peeved Callie was ten minutes late to our session. While I was sympathetic to her busy work schedule, I was eager for her to make the best use of our time together. "You can't make babies without taking baby steps."

Callie didn't protest. Instead she listened as I explained that even if Jake or Mike or Jennifer didn't end up being the perfect match for her, I could learn a lot from her interactions with them—observations and judgments that could help lead me closer to finding her person. If she really wanted me to do that, I needed her to start going on actual dates, and soon.

"They can come from anywhere, though," I reminded her. "You don't have to meet someone through my database, although obviously that would make me happy. But I'm not just your matchmaker—I'm also your dating coach. And I can give you the tools needed to meet the right person, whether that's through a friend or at the supermarket. But you have to stop judging people and start getting to know them, okay? Which means actually meeting them." Callie nodded.

I had emailed her about my agenda for today's session on online dating, and she seemed receptive to—or at least curious about—what I had to say on the subject. Some singles view apps as the antithesis to matchmaking, but the truth is, a good matchmaker should encourage their clients to supplement their dating life in as many ways as possible. Even if the quality of our matches is generally higher than what's "out there," we only know so many people. Besides, if I could help arm Callie with the skills needed to recognize, and not accidentally overlook, the right match on her own, I'd still be a meaningful part of her journey to find love—which was all I really cared about.

Callie wasn't the biggest fan of online dating, which I understood. These platforms boast a wide range of options, but in some ways, they're also quite restrictive: 10 to 15 percent of bachelors and bachelorettes will receive more than 90 percent of the likes, a phenomenon dating app employees refer to as "hypergamy." (This behavior occurs in person too. Lauren and I once threw a "game night" for clients so they could meet more than one potential love interest simultaneously, but instead of everyone getting to know each other, all the bachelors and bachelorettes flocked toward the same one or two people they deemed the most "desirable"—usually for superficial reasons. As a result, they were overlooking people they might really have connected with otherwise, and now we couldn't set them up, because they already knew each other. We stopped throwing singles mixers.) There's also data breaches, invasive advertising, safety concerns, and sexual harassment to worry about. According to a Pew survey conducted in 2023, women are more likely to have negative experiences on dating apps than men. "About two-thirds of women under 50 said they had received physical threats, experienced unwanted continued contact from a match, been called an offensive name or been sent unsolicited sexual messages or images."

There is also a leading provider of dating services that threatens innovation, which most certainly impacts quality. Match Group holds almost 50 percent of the global market, with their vast empire overseeing more than forty dating companies—including some of the most popular ones: Tinder, Hinge, OkCupid, and The League. While these apps are "designed to be deleted" (Hinge's slogan), these companies are incentivized to keep you on them for as long as possible—after all, more monthly subscribers means more profit for their shareholders. This strategy is made easier by literal dopamine rushes (or surges of the "feel good" hormone) whenever users get notified of new matches, and discounts for paying for a bulk of time up front. (In her Netflix comedy special *Single Lady*, Ali Wong mentions she almost missed out on a relationship because she'd just spent $250 on an annual subscription to a dating app and wanted to get her "money's worth.") There's also a "gamified" experience that promotes an endless variety of new matches over deepening connections with current ones. The result for many is often superficial conversation that rarely leads to actual dates.

The existence of AI also throws a wrench into an already difficult-to-navigate landscape. Determining which strangers are quality people worth investing in was already a tough endeavor, but now, many people use AI to help boost their profiles or conversation, leading some singles to feel deceived after meeting their dates in person. Tools such as ChatGPT, or even an app such as Rizz, can help people come off as wittier or more charming than they actually are. Others are aware they're chatting with AI, but that doesn't always stop them from connecting emotionally with it. On AI chatbot apps like Replika, users can create and interact with AI companions, including romantic partners. And these relationships can have detrimental consequences beyond unhealthy attachments. A Belgian environmentalist wound up committing suicide after his chatbot, Eliza, convinced him to sacrifice himself to save the planet. (AI also offers positives with online dating, such as Bumble's "Private Detector," a tool that blurs explicit images, and their "Deception Detector," which identifies fake profiles—but the downsides are hard to overlook.)

Despite these challenges, there was no denying online dating was still, statistically, the easiest way to meet someone. "But my guy would never use an app," some clients tell me. *Really?* I ask. Even if it's not in their nature, after a decade or so of not meeting the One, eventually they might try using it, and don't you want to be "findable" when that happens?

I don't intend to dismiss "the burnout," because online dating—equivalent to having another full-time job—is an absolute mind suck. But it's important to stick with it, even if that means leaving your profile active while taking a two- or three-week break and catching up on your messages later; or even having a friend "run" your profile for you. I don't recommend a friend pretending to *be* you, which could start off a potential relationship on the wrong foot. Instead, I recommend a friend "taking over" your profile, explaining who they are and why they want to find a match for you. This tactic isn't overused yet, and is a refreshing way to possibly add new blood to the mix with little to no effort on your part. Plus, your friend, if single, could benefit—just as my friend and Benicio del Toro's former assistant Jackie did. When she "took over" a friend's dating profile, she wound up meeting *her* now husband, an upbeat, Italian manufacturing engineer, Sergio, instead. Initially, Jackie showed her friend Sergio's picture, but the friend wasn't interested in meeting him. So Jackie threw her own hat in the ring, and now she and Sergio are married with a newborn. I shared this story with Callie, who lit up at this creative approach to dating.

She felt open-minded after our pep talk, and we brainstormed about the best app for her to start with. Bumble is helpful if you're in need of good conversation starters; J-Swipe, Christian Mingle, or Catholic Match are strong examples that make dating within your own religion easier (BLK, Kyank, or Dil Mil are solid options within specific races); Grindr and HER are popular among the LGBTQ+ community; and The League is a good resource if you're tired of the bartenders and struggling actors populating your feed. Coffee Meets Bagel works best for AAPI males, Match.com or eHarmony for singles over fifty, and Raya for fun dating tales starring Marvel superheroes and famous drummers (or if you want to get away with not listing your height). I'm not as much of a fan of the ones that limit swiping, within reason, as it should be up to each individual to demonstrate restraint.

All of these trends have the capacity to ebb and flow, but I encouraged Callie to start with the one I felt consistently hosts the highest-quality singles on it, Hinge (and the paid version, so she could more easily narrow down her search criteria). It has many prompts to choose from, is user-friendly, and what's written there can usually be applied to all the other apps in case a change is later desired.

She screen-shared her profile. I hoped that by going through it, I could finally gain more insight into what she was truly searching for, and help her attract that more easily.

The way to win me over is

By surprising me, whether it's with a home-cooked meal (even if it isn't good!) or tickets to my favorite band.

Typical Sunday

Peloton or pickleball, brunch with my friends, squeezing in some work, and maybe a stand-up comedy show.

The dorkiest thing about me is

My obsession with Meg White.

I suggested that when we were done updating everything, she should launch her new profile under an alternate email address. If she hadn't received optimal engagement from users before, more coveted profiles wouldn't be shown to her now. For the first time since we started working together, I saw Callie take out her note-book.

Looking her profile over again, I immediately identified ways she could make better use of the limited real estate provided to her. Swipers subconsciously want to know whether they can envision fitting into your life, but they can't do that if they're unsure who you are. Based on what Callie had shared about herself, she appeared to be active, playful, social, and driven. But she defined herself almost entirely by what she liked to do for fun. Perhaps unsurprising, most singles tend to lead with this information, believing it will make them appear more interesting, or that someone might want to connect with them over a mutual interest—but it could also backfire, accidentally alienating someone with different passions.

"*I just returned from Gabon,*" a client once wrote in her intake. "*And tracked the elusive African Forest Elephant, in the dense, humid jungle, on foot. I traveled to the Yangtze River in China to glimpse the Yangtze Finless Porpoise, the only living freshwater porpoise in the world. And to help protect the Hawksbill Turtle, I encouraged fisheries to switch to more turtle-friendly fishing hooks. I've been to more than fifty countries, and still counting.*" This was fascinating information, but what did it really say about her? Did she go searching for endangered wildlife for the thrill of it? To check something off her bucket list? Or did she simply love animals? The why, and not the what, would be more revealing about her character. Bonding over shared interests is a bonus, but remember: Hobbies can be acquired. Shared values and life goals, on the other hand, are far more indicative of long-term compatibility.

"So, what would you change?" Callie finally asked bravely about her profile. "I can handle it."

"Well, for starters, you spend the first prompt talking about the way someone can win you over, which would be fine if that actually helped weed out the wrong people. But realistically, anyone who finds you attractive is going to try to match with you, whether or not they fit the description of what you're looking for. So it ends up being a waste of space and time. You want prompt responses that focus on *you*."

Rather than dive in more immediately, I suggested I get to know her even better first. I asked her to ignore the prompts provided, and wondered aloud what she would want her future husband or wife to know about her. Once she knew what she wanted to share about herself, we could reverse-engineer that into her profile. "This isn't about getting as many likes as possible," I reminded her. "It's about attracting the right person, and getting them to engage more once that happens."

I could sense she was starting to feel overwhelmed. "Let me put it another way," I added after she struggled to answer. "What would your best friend or mom say sets you apart?"

Callie laughed. "My mom would say I'm scaring people off. She says I intimidate them."

"Intimidate how?"

"Well, I was captain of a kickball league once," Callie shared. "She told me I was never gonna find someone yelling at teammates to round third."

"So you're a little bossy. That's perfect. Also, your mom is wrong." A future partner would likely find her kickball story endearing. "In fact, you should add it to your profile."

"That my mom thinks I'll die alone?"

"That you were captain of a kickball team," I said fondly. "And you were more interested in winning than the free drinks afterward. That's who you are, and that's the kind of thing that will get your future partner's attention. They may or may not care that you're also into The White Stripes."

"Oh, they'll care." She smiled. I could tell she was pleased that I'd recognized the reference in her earlier prompt response. "I get it, though," she added. "Fewer hobbies and interests, more personal stories that showcase who I am."

"Exactly." Specificity matters too. I shared that I was much more interested in her being captain of a kickball team, for example, than her riding the Peloton along with every other suburban woman in America. I thought about all my other clients who listed "brunching, traveling, and watching TV" without realizing just how generic it made them all sound. They'd be much better off offering some insight into their life and personality. *What were their favorite brunch spots, and why? Did they travel home to visit family, or choose a destination based on its number of Michelin stars? And if "watching TV" was such a big part of their life, what shows were they into?* Again, think the *why* and not the *what*.

"Tell me more," I challenged Callie. "You're playfully bossy, with good leadership skills. What about a softer side, that only those close to you get to see? I know you have it."

"That doesn't mean I want thousands of strangers knowing too."

"Maybe not. But you want at least one of them to. Right? And you've got a much better chance at that if they get to see who you really are. You're a good person, but how so? Pretend I'm a judge. What's your evidence?"

"I don't know. My friends and family think I am?"

"Okay. So, what would they say on the witness stand? My best friend drops matzo ball soup at my doorstep whenever I'm sick," I used as an example.

"Hmmm. I drive friends to the airport? And that's saying a lot." (She referenced LAX, the stuff traffic nightmares are made of.) "I volunteer at an animal shelter."

"You do?" I responded, somewhat surprised. "See? I'm learning about you already."

She also shared that she calls her grandmother every week. I banged the pretend gavel, demonstrating a case won.

"What are you waiting for?" I instructed. "Put it in your profile!"

When she was done, I summarized our conversation. She included the kickball bit, which showed she was active and funny. The airport and grandma stuff proved she had a good heart. Still, her profile was missing one more component.

"Can I leave in Meg White?" she interrupted. "Please?"

"Sure." I smiled. "You can leave in Meg White."

I was happy to see her satisfied with how the session was going, but we were far from done. I turned to the "voice" portion of her profile.

"How you share information is equally important," I added. "Saying you're funny, for example, is different than telling a joke. You could be witty, deeply insightful, or the smartest woman on Hinge. But right now, your profile could use more personality."

To help her address that, I ran through a series of questions. *Are you more sarcastic or cheesy? Bashful or boastful? Do you like to pontificate or get straight to the point? Do you tend to use more slang, or do you consider yourself more formal?* She admitted she never really thought about all this before, and I assured her that was normal. But it was necessary that we capture her essence if we were going to attract the right person.

"And remember," I added, "you're not a monolith—you can be playful and serious, all at the same time. Don't be afraid to display a range."

I used Meg White as an example, suggesting we include the same information about her obsession, but use it as an opportunity to display another facet of herself, such as her willingness to compromise. "Take the '*What if I told you*' prompt"—I referenced one of Hinge's conversational lead-ins. "What if I told you that I'd go to any concert you like if you let me play the White Stripes on our road trip?" Callie nodded, digesting. "See how you're giving similar information, but doing it in a way that highlights who you are a bit more?"

"Well, it highlights who *you* are." She grinned amusedly.

Like she was in her initial Zoom with me, Callie had been positive and generally good-natured all session, and I couldn't help but wonder where this version of her had been hiding the last two months. I felt optimistic things were about to take a turn, and I had to give her credit: she was taking my criticism like a champ.

Feeling I still had her attention, I shifted the conversation to what prompts to respond to. (A Hinge expert once shared the "54 Best Hinge-Prompt Answers," and I had to laugh—how is sharing the 54 best anything supposed to help guide someone? My list was much narrower.)

As an extension of our conversation before, I suggested eliminating any that put the focus on the other person. I also steered her away from negative prompts such as "*You should not go out with me if . . .*" or "*Something that's nonnegotiable for me is . . .*" Putting a positive spin on your wants is important. You don't want to come off pessimistic. Another useless prompt is "*Two truths and a lie.*" (I get a lot of pushback on this one, because it's often the prompt that elicits the most engagement from other swipers. But ask yourself: Is this engagement from the *right* swipers? Or did you simply present a fun "game" people were interested in playing? While it's a fun conversation starter, one of your three "facts" listed isn't even real. If you're going to attempt it, at least be sure that your truths are more compelling than your lie.) Being straightforward about who you are will usually be more appealing to the right person.

I encouraged Callie to use one of my personal favorites: "*The one thing you should know about me is . . . ,*" "*Biggest risk I've taken,*" or "*My greatest strength.*" I also recommended prompts that spoke to life goals, since that's something that can be shared with the person reading it. "*Together we could . . . ,*" "*A life goal of mine is . . . ,*" and "*This year, I really want to . . .*" are some favorites. I'm also into creative openers such as "*Weirdest gift I've ever given or received,*" "*My most controversial opinion,*" and "*Apparently my life's soundtrack is . . .*" They're all layups to show off your playful side. But if you can find another way to convey that within the body of a more seriously framed question, you'll not only demonstrate your wit but also reveal another, more vulnerable side of yourself in the process—something I was eager for Callie to do.

(Since conducting my session with Callie, Hinge partnered with psychotherapist and *New York Times* bestselling author Esther Perel to create additional prompts. All ten of hers, which fall under the category "Your World" and range from "*I could stay up all night talking about . . .*" to "*Something my pet thinks about me*" are 100 percent Jaydi approved!)

My lesson wasn't over yet, though. We figured out what Callie wanted to say, and how to say it, but the order of it all was equally important. If she began her profile too intensely, she could scare off the right match.

"I like to think about moving through your profile the same way you should date: starting off light, then getting a bit more serious and vulnerable as someone gets to know you better." I shuffled things around a moment and pulled up the updated version:

The dorkiest thing about me is

I was captain of my kickball team (and I was more interested in winning than the free drinks afterward).

What if I told you that

I'd go to any concert you like if you let me play The White Stripes on our road trip?

The one thing you should know about me is

I call my grandma Sue every week.

I also advised her to make her desire for a long-term relationship visible, so she could filter out the people just looking to hook up.

Callie agreed, then asked my opinion on her photos. I'd been worried about inundating her, but she was eager for more feedback. I wondered whether she was a glutton for punishment or my best student yet. I reviewed her photos again, and answered truthfully that they were really strong. They were well lit, and she clearly knew her angles well. I typically start with pictures when doing profile punch-ups, because while online dating tends to be superficial, so is actual dating. (At a party, someone is unlikely to approach you because of your kindness and intelligence, since those traits aren't visible.) Most daters are used to starting with the physical, because often that's all you can go by, and the same holds true digitally. I suggested that she make the photo of her smiling her main one since it was the most inviting.

Approachability is a key part of the process. I once worked with a video game designer who wouldn't swipe right on any woman not smiling, because, often wrongfully, he assumed she was too serious. He's not alone in that assumption, though. Callie had a nice mix of close-ups and full-body shots, which was key. Daters often assume, in the absence of one or the other, that someone is hiding something. Photos in sunglasses, hats, or any other accessories that might obscure what a person actually looks like are another common mistake, but her shots didn't have them. Nor were her photos overly filtered.

"I love the one with your girlfriends," I noted to her, impressed. "It shows you're social. And you chose a good one where you're the main focal point." So many daters recognize the value in sharing a group shot without realizing that including someone else more traditionally attractive than they are might inadvertently turn matches off. Who wants to date you knowing they might have the hots for your friend instead?

"If I switched out anything," I added, purposely nitpicking, "I'd say the last two are a little redundant." Both photos, clearly taken on the same day, featured her in the same floral dress. I advised her to swap one with another of her in action, on a hike or on a trip—making it more tempting for a swiper to envision themselves in her life.

I also encouraged her to make use of the captions, another way to capitalize on available real estate. Utilizing the space would make Callie stand out more, offering a potential match more useful information about her personality and outlook.

Lastly, I steered her away from recording a voice prompt. Like the disappointment you feel when a movie character sounds nothing like the one you envisioned when reading the book, you don't want someone to write you off because your voice doesn't match the way they imagined it sounding. Callie had a nice voice, but someone would discover that soon enough in person—while also getting to know the whole package. Swipers are constantly looking for reasons to reject people, so don't give them one more reason to say no.

"I wasn't really sure how this was going to go," Callie admitted to me. "But this has been great."

I beamed back at her, pleased she was getting something out of our time together.

"By the way," I added before we wrapped, "if you ever get bored or feel stuck, I'm also a fan of scoping out the competition."

"The 'competition'?" she repeated, baffled.

"The other men and women competing for the same dates. I wouldn't do it for too long, because it'll mess with your algorithm—but for a few minutes or so, change your settings to search for people like you. You can see how others in a similar demographic are 'selling themselves.' Might give you some ideas."

"Wow. That's kind of genius."

I glanced at the clock. We only had a few minutes left, but this was the part I'd been looking forward to the most, and my covert agenda for today's session: gaining more insight into what she was truly searching for by swiping together. Given her hasty dismissals of my carefully vetted "nominees," I was curious who, in her eyes, passed muster. And so I watched. Unlike friends and clients with analysis paralysis, Callie was swiping through matches left and right, categorically ruling out people with decent potential in mere seconds. I gently asked her to walk me through her logic.

"Well, this guy wears too much hair gel," she commented readily, or "This one's eyebrows are too distracting. How could I ever focus on what he's saying? Oh, and see here?" She stopped on a good-looking guy wearing a baseball cap. "Classic hat-fisher," she said, referring to some men's attempts to mask a receding hairline or bad haircut with certain angles or headwear. While she had a point—it's better for a man to own that kind of thing rather than to catch his date off guard—on the whole, I felt that such strong opinions and reactions up front were unreasonable.

"You know he can quit once he has kids, right?" I referred to the skydiver she was about to reject based on his pastime.

"Fine. But take this chick . . ." She scrolled through a woman's profile skeptically. "Cute enough, right? But she's a VP in business affairs."

"So?"

"So she should be an SVP by now. At her age?"

I held up my hand, forcing her to slow down. "What if she switched professions later in life? What if she's the most charming woman you've ever met who nursed her sick mother back to health and wants kids next year?" I looked at her with genuine curiosity. Overly focusing on someone's financials is usually a mistake—but if it has to be done, I typically encourage clients to think more about their partner's earning potential rather than their current income. That kind of selectivity was leaving no room for nuance. What if a person was laid off right before you met them? Or something unexpected happened and they were forced to drain their life savings? These things could happen five minutes into a relationship, or fifteen years into one.

"I can't believe you did it," Callie told me before we ran out of time.

"Did what?"

"Convinced me to stay on the apps."

I was relieved, and wondered if after all this time, I had finally earned her trust.

THE MIDPOINT (AKA THE INEVITABLE STEP BACKWARD)

"I . . . feel . . . like . . . the . . . worst . . . person . . . ever." Meera was still sobbing a few minutes into our session and I wanted to provide a safe space—even if that meant watching in silence—as she gathered her thoughts. When she finally came up for air, she managed to share that she ended up meeting Raj, the guy she'd been talking to on Bumble, but apparently the whole ordeal had been wildly disappointing, and she was still questioning whether or not she emotionally cheated on Trevor—despite their relationship not yet being exclusive. Currently Trevor had all the benefits of being in a relationship with her, but with none of the responsibilities, such as lending emotional support or being present for important events. Her anxiety surrounding all of this might have been avoided if she had actually been attracted to Raj, but she was unwilling to see if that could change.

Attraction can grow sometimes—think of any friend you've ever slowly fallen for—however, Meera was used to fireworks on night one. It's not that you can't, or shouldn't, have them, but I also know dozens of happy couples whose chemistry continued to build over time, and neither scenario is "better" than the other. That's not to say I believe in giving people two or three dates no matter what, though. While an extra date is helpful if you're on the fence about someone—whether that's after one date or after dating for one year—I do believe you can be certain someone *isn't* your person, even after a first impression. If you don't get a glimpse of something that could convince you otherwise, you should walk away. Reacting with disgust when you first meet someone is an unlikely recipe for a lifelong romance. Trying to make that work potentially wastes valuable time—time you could be meeting someone else better suited to you.

Meera had experienced glimpses of potential with Raj, though. That seed of a connection, in my opinion, warranted at least one more date to see whether her initial feelings for him would grow. In nature, a tree won't sprout in the middle of nowhere, but if a seed exists, it's possible to water it and give it enough sunlight until a sapling appears. Meera wasn't interested in doing that, likely because she was comparing her first date with Raj to her first date with Trevor—ignoring the fact that it's been somewhat downhill with him ever since.

"Am I the most hopeless client you've ever worked with?" Meera asked defeatedly.

I didn't answer: not because I was unsure, but because my screen froze at the absolute worst moment, just as I was about to comfort her. But my contorted face had the desirable effect of making her laugh, which immediately cut all the tension. As I gracefully recovered, I shared my perspective that this complication brought on by Raj was good for Meera's growth. Although her dalliance with him didn't go as planned, she put herself out there, and was able to imagine an alternate, positive reality from the one she was living. I wished she could see the benefits of that, but right now, she was too terrified Trevor would find the previous messages from Raj on her phone, find out she went on a date with another man, and somehow hold that against her.

Once I felt she had the emotional bandwidth, I tackled her accidental admission. What would Trevor be doing on her phone anyway? Was he the jealous type? Did she feel the need to share her password with him to demonstrate trust? Transparency is important in any good relationship, but so is the existence of boundaries. From what I could tell, Meera didn't have many in her relationships, whether that was with friends, family members, or romantic entanglements. She feared that in setting them, she'd push people away. This insecurity caused her to want to feel chosen rather than actively doing the choosing.

I asked whether she noticed the pattern. She did, but her next declaration threw me: she said her therapist told her that her suffering in love was all due to "past-life regression." I took a deep breath. When she'd told me she'd been seeing a therapist, I didn't think to ask what kind. I have limited knowledge about this particular type of metaphysical trauma (and, full disclosure, I'm skeptical it actually exists—it's been widely discredited in the scientific community), but my understanding is that it's based on the idea that emotions and experiences from past lives affect our current behavior. Through hypnotherapy, a person can supposedly confront their deeply rooted fears and anxiety, and this was something Meera had been exploring.

I tried to keep an open mind as she told me more (a good friend had tried this method once, and I do admit she demonstrated undeniable growth afterward). During one hypnotherapy session, Meera had learned that in a past life, she'd taken a vow to never marry again after her lover died during an early medieval battle in India. To break the cycle of her misfortune in love, her therapist said Meera would have to give herself permission to break her vow. I'm normally all for breaking cycles, but I strongly believed Meera was unlucky in love because she was choosing the wrong men, not because of a tenth-century curse. As Meera described more of Trevor's bad behavior—most recently, that he hadn't called her in two days following a "silly" argument of theirs—I wanted to remind her that we weren't in early medieval India now, and this mess was of Trevor's own making, as well as her own. I knew that effort would be futile, though. So instead, I listened.

"He said it again," she told me, referring to the L-word.

"Oh?" I replied evenly. "How did it happen?"

"Well, he called me 'love,'" she clarified earnestly. "He said, 'I'll see you soon, love,' when he hung up last week, before our fight. That's a good step, right?"

I tried my best to project optimism. The term of endearment can be uplifting when attached to corresponding action, but the latter half was missing.

"How did that make you feel?" I asked instead, cringing as the most cliché of all coaching questions left my lips.

She admitted it made her feel confused. "If I'm really his 'love,'" she started to reason, "I don't get why he treats me this way. Or only wants to see me once a week."

I asked whether she'd expressed to him that she'd like to see *him* more often. She said she had, but he'd told her that it was tough with work. I had to weigh my advice. Some people genuinely do have challenging schedules that make carving out quality time difficult, but when someone is a priority, even busy people will usually find other ways to express their affection—and I wasn't sure Trevor had done that. I also wasn't sure if Trevor had any idea how much his inconsistent behavior dysregulated Meera, or whether he could tell, but didn't care.

"Maybe I'll just be less responsive to him and see how he likes it," Meera announced.

I grimaced at her impulse to give Trevor a taste of his own medicine. I'm all for modeling behavior with a partner, but more so when that behavior is affirming. If you want your romantic interest to call you instead of text, for example, then *you* call them first. If you want your partner to initiate more affection, then you're to do the same. These actions typically yield positive results, even more so when paired with a light conversation surrounding the topic (e.g., "Talking on the phone makes me feel more connected to you"). But Meera told Trevor she'd like to see him more, and he hadn't modified his behavior as a result.

"He also hasn't suggested an alternative to make you feel more comfortable," I pointed out to her.

"No. But he's telling me how much he misses me when I see him. And he says he's never met anyone like me before." I sighed. *More heightened language without the corresponding follow-through. Trevor, what are you doing? And, more important, what is Meera doing?*

Buzz. Trevor texted Meera during our Zoom, and her face

instantly lit up. I told her I was concerned she was hanging on to any kind of positive reinforcement from him as a sign he was still interested in her, and she looked crestfallen.

"But he is. Isn't he?"

"He is," I admitted reluctantly. "But is he interested enough?" She wiped away a tear that had slid down her cheek, which was difficult to watch. Delivering hard truths is part of my job, but sometimes it makes me feel like *I'm* the one hurting someone rather than their partner. "You're a special person," I reminded her how I saw her. "You feel deeply, you're passionate, intelligent, and warm, with an incredible circle of family and friends. I know you feel something between you and Trevor, and I believe it's there. But while I can't see the future, I don't think the right man for you will make you cry. At least not this early, and this often."

I'd been dancing around the conclusion that I'd hoped for some time Meera would arrive at on her own, but one of us needed to say it aloud—if only for her to hear what it sounded like. "I'm saying all this because I care. Even if Trevor suddenly starts calling you his girlfriend, or proposes to you one day, none of those labels are going to change his emotional unavailability."

Meera nodded. She didn't disagree—how could she? But it didn't mean she was ready to walk away from him yet. If I bullied her into doing it before she was ready, then I'd be no better than Trevor. Meera was busy with work coming up, and asked if we could meet again in a month. That was perfect for me. The space would give Meera time to digest our conversation, and with everything going on lately, I'd hoped to carve out some more quality time with Dave.

I wondered how Meera would fare the next month between our sessions. I was frustrated with her for not seeing the signs with Trevor, but then again, maybe I needed to start paying more attention to my own. This IVF business had been impacting my energy around Dave—needles, bruising, and failed medical procedures hadn't exactly been the world's best aphrodisiacs. And I wondered if we simply weren't meant to have biological children. How many times had I returned for more treatments despite receiving discouraging results? What if the failed embryo transfer and abnormal test results we were getting were signs that it was time for us to stop trying? What signs are we supposed to pay attention to, and which ones do we ignore in order to achieve our desired outcome?

I was putting myself through all this for a reason, I told myself, and was certain Meera was doing the same thing. I hoped at least one of us was right.

LOCATION, LOCATION, LOCATION!

The following month, I woke up to an email from Claire, a vibrant photographer I'd been working with on and off for the past few years. Lauren and I had set her up with her previous boyfriend, but when things didn't work out with them, she'd resurfaced, wondering whether we had anyone else in mind for her. I told her about Jim, a self-assured and athletic talent agent, hoping they'd hit it off. According to her feedback after the date, she found him "cute and easy to talk to," but she had objections.

"*Sure, he's successful,*" she wrote, "*but he was ten minutes late, talked a little too much about his achievements, and was a bit of a name-dropper, so that hinted he could be a little immature or ego driven. He had also just recovered from a Ritalin-fueled fifty-hour work streak. All in all, decent conversationalist, bad lifestyle fit.*"

Oh, Jim. I sighed, annoyed—at Jim for not getting his act together, and at Claire for not seeing their potential in spite of it. But, more than anything, I was annoyed at myself for sending them to Petty Cash Taqueria. Despite its convenient location and rightful title as one of LA's "mezcal hot spots," the restaurant had barely produced any second dates between my clients. I vowed to stop sending people there, a promise I'd forgotten with everything else I'd been juggling lately.

I silently reprimanded myself for the error. After all, I'd taken the time to sort through years of previous date statistics involving my clients—out of sheer curiosity and perhaps too much time on my hands—and knew offhand which restaurants were most likely to yield second dates for singles, and which ones likely interfered with that process. After recognizing some undeniable patterns, I started taking clients' feedback on date settings as seriously as their chemistry with their matches.

What kind of service, food, or ambiance is most effective for finding love? After a while, the data seemed to speak for itself. For starters, *great parking*. If someone spends twenty minutes searching for a spot, or begrudgingly dishes out for overpriced valet, their energy coming into the date is more likely to be negative. Petty Cash happened to be located on a busy street where finding good parking was tricky. Viviane at the Avalon Hotel, however, was less trendy, but offered free valet for anyone dining at their establishment. I suspected that the bachelors I sent there for drinks regularly left with firm plans to see their dates again in large part due to the convenience and ease of the parking experience without the added price tag.

I've also found that privacy, but not too much of it, matters. Petty Cash featured communal tables: great for people-watching and striking up conversation with strangers, but less conducive to creating a rapport with one person. (I hate dates when couples sit at bars for this reason. Some people believe the casualness of the bar seats will be disarming for their matches, but the close proximity to others can backfire. Instead of focusing on their date's wit, charisma, or kindness, people can be so preoccupied by who might be watching or eavesdropping that they aren't present for the conversation.) When booking reservations, you should consider an actual table where outside influences aren't a factor. If a table is *too* private, though, awkward silences are more apparent, and diners lose the ability to gossip about those around them—a vital crutch when a conversation stalls (e.g., *Are those people one table over on a date too or having drinks with a coworker? Is that woman in the corner waiting for her date to show up? Or is she an escort?*).

The noise factor is also a consideration. Whether a spot is blasting a cool, rock-inspired soundtrack (Petty Cash was named after Tom Petty and Johnny Cash, respectively, so the music was always top-notch) or bustling with activity, a balance needs to exist between hearing your date and feeling like you're at a happening location.

Airflow is also commonly overlooked. Even outside a health context, I find that airflow has become a measurable part of someone's comfort level and prompts a whole new set of questions: *Is a patio there? Are you comfortable? How's the view?* When the weather's nice, I often schedule first dates at rooftop locations to take all of those concerns off the table.

I've also learned that regardless of how desirable a venue might be, switching it up is important. In my early years of arranging dates, I'd send clients to the first places that would populate my Open Table or Resy accounts, not tracking whether a client had been there before. It might have been an innocent inconvenience the first few times, creating a sense of an unpleasant routine, but it deprived them and their new date of the joy of experiencing something new together. (I have select clients who thrive in familiar settings, so for them, I tend to rotate among the same three or four places.)

I started to consider all of it, and spiral more about Jim and Claire—whose date didn't even sound that bad. Was their poor connection really a result of my restaurant choice (it pained me I would never know), or had they been a doomed match from the start? I'd been certain the two would have instant chemistry or, at the very least, enough interest to make it to date two. Aside from being each other's ideal physical type, I thought Claire would find Jim charming and intelligent, and that her even-keeled temperament would balance him out well. He was edgier than the men she normally dated, but successful and grounded (at least when he got enough sleep).

As I closed Claire's email, I wondered if either of them had at least enjoyed the restaurant's highly acclaimed aguachile.

As I entered my office after lunch, I was hoping Callie could help turn my day around, which was a lot to ask from a client who had yet to give me a win. We were meeting shortly to discuss her date with Ethan, a promising VFX company owner and database member I set her up with. During her recap, she claimed to be "unexpectedly attracted to his long hair and painted black nails," and loved that his teddy bear personality "didn't quite match his more punk appearance." She also said she appreciated his emotional and financial stability, and the fact that he seemed ready to have kids. But she'd already told him she wasn't interested in another date, and I couldn't imagine why.

"He's from the same hometown as my ex," she revealed in the opening moments of our session, as if that was an obvious disqualifier.

"Where's that?" I couldn't remember off the top of my head, and pictured some sort of small-town rivalry between Ethan and one of Callie's ex-boyfriends, stemming from dating the same bachelorette from a neighboring Midwest farm in high school or something.

"Miami," she replied coolly.

My head nearly exploded. "Wait, you won't go out with him again because he's from Miami? Am I supposed to rule out anyone who happens to be from the Greater Miami area?" I posed the question slowly, in case she was forgetting the nearly half million people who live there.

"Well, not necessarily," she attempted to backtrack, but I could already tell the answer was yes.

Carefully and calmly, I looked for opportunities to ask more about her dating history, hoping to receive clues about her avoidant behavior. Before long, I learned more about her most serious ex, whom she broke up with over children. Both had wanted them, but he preferred to wait a few more years, once he was more established professionally. Callie had wanted to try conceiving within one year of meeting him, and a few years felt too long to wait. She told me this was four years ago, without acknowledging the mathematical irony.

"He's married now with a kid. But you know what?" She conjectured, "If he was meant for me, my timeline would have worked for him."

The confidence with which she said it surprised me. It's not often that you hear someone deliver such a clear opinion on something so ambiguous. But then, I realized: she came to that conclusion because she had to. The alternative—that she'd messed up, and might have wound up with a great guy had she only been more patient with him—might have been too much for her to accept.

Timing is a huge point of contention in the dating community. Some people believe that it matters on a near-cosmic level. Others think it's just what you make of it. "Boo Boo would have been right for me whether we met now or when we were kids," my best friend used to insist about her now ex-husband. I, however, couldn't be more certain that Dave and I would have butted heads when we were younger. I'd have labeled him a "stoner hippie," and he'd have called me a "giant nerd," a designation he now uses as a term of endearment. We'd since had the same conversations as Callie and her ex about what our respective timelines looked like in terms of children and other major milestones, and for us, the topics had been tough to navigate.

After we got married, Dave wanted to start trying for kids immediately. Being younger than him, I felt less pressure and, like Callie's ex, wanted more time to grow my career before launching into yet another life phase. We had gotten engaged after only ten months, and there was so much more I wanted us to do together before taking on additional responsibilities, like attend a music festival or visit Australia. Dave implored me to reconsider: he really didn't want to be an "old dad." He was in his early forties, and in his mind, prone to imagining worst-case scenarios, he was going to die before our kid graduated high school. Truthfully, I didn't want Dave to be an "old dad" either. Being the only one of us with enough energy to chase around a toddler wasn't exactly an appealing scenario for me.

Through our wonderful therapist, Dr. Christopher Walling, Dave and I came to realize that there was no such thing as a "his" and "hers" timeline—at least not in a healthy relationship. While I came into ours with preconceived notions about when I wanted to have kids, Dave was the partner I wanted to have them with, and with that came certain realities such as his age. By considering us as a *unit*, rather than myself as an individual, I discovered his timeline was actually *ours*. (And it's a good thing we started when we did, given our need for fertility assistance.)

Now that Callie was older, her desire to have kids was playing a larger role in her dating life, but it was leading to its own form of self-sabotage—her negative and intense energy counteracting her end goal of making a lasting romantic connection. Rather than explore her potential with a match organically, she was making dates feel more like interviews, and alienating potential life partners, and baby daddies, as a result. When I'd asked Ethan his thoughts on Callie, he replied that she was attractive and interesting, but also intense.

"She asked about my medical history, eating habits, and timeline," he told me in confidence. "I felt like she was more interested in my sperm than me."

I felt for Callie. I understood why she was interested in this information, but could also see how, for Ethan—and most matches simply looking for a relaxed, light conversation on date one—it might have felt uncomfortable. While I'm typically annoyed when men "request" younger women for their setups, for every guy who does so, there's typically a jaded woman in a rush who once turned him off from other women her age.

"Tell me about your parents," I pivoted.

"I don't talk to my dad." Callie shrugged, as if this were no big deal. "My parents had a great marriage, or at least I thought they did. Until he fucked the intern. Don't worry, though," she reassured me quickly. "I've covered this plenty already in therapy." I smiled to indicate I wasn't worried at all. In fact, her disclosure had offered more clarity than I'd gotten at any point in the process so far. That she was having trouble allowing romantic prospects to get close to her after watching her own parents' marriage fall apart made sense now. The most important male figure in her life had revealed himself to be untrustworthy in a relationship. Carefully, I asked whether she could picture herself having a more successful partnership than her parents had, and she struggled to answer.

"Allowing your mind to go there's important," I encouraged. "I'd give different advice if you didn't truly want to be loved the way you deserve, or if you really believe that it's not in the cards for you. But I don't think you'd be here if any of that were true." I gave her a moment to process that somewhat complicated truth. "I want to introduce you to someone amazing, the kind of person I know you dream about. But you can't just say you want that. You have to take the steps necessary to make it happen—and that means giving people a chance, even if they're from Miami. Or wear way too much hair gel."

"Or don't use social media," she added playfully. "But seriously, who doesn't have an Instagram account these days?"

I breathed a sigh of relief. The Callie I first met was back. "I don't know . . . serial killers, loners, Jennifer Lawrence, and some busy CEOs?" I responded cheekily.

"Jennifer Lawrence doesn't use socials?" Callie looked incredulous.

"I don't think so. But see how quickly a possible red flag turned into a beige one?" I asked.

This felt like a good place to wrap up our session. We'd gotten into some pretty heavy subject matter, and I was glad that things were ending on a more lighthearted note. Before we parted, Callie admitted that although it didn't work out with Ethan, higher-quality men and women had been messaging her on dating apps ever since we tweaked her profile. "All that's left to do is reply to them," she said hopefully.

And for a moment, I believed her.

THE HALLMARK VACATION

I've never been a big drinker, but Solvang—a quaint town in the Santa Ynez Valley, known for its many vineyards—holds a special place in my heart. Dave had suggested we visit there our first winter together: two Jews frolicking through Danish windmills, Hans Christian Andersen statues, and Christmas tree lighting ceremonies in the "Tijuana of Denmark" (a backhanded term of endearment, bestowed by my friend's mom). We had a blast, and have made it our go-to drivable getaway spot ever since. Now, four months after our embryo transfer fail, a trip there felt like a great idea. We'd be able to decompress, spend time together, and block out the rest of the world. At least that was the plan, but as we drove into town, I thought of Kent's winery, which was only twenty minutes away.

"I'll give you the VIP experience," he'd promised once, but I wasn't sure I wanted our romantic trip to get hijacked by another lesson from Kent on grape cultivation, or more questions about Natasha.

Kent resurfaced recently, almost two months following his sudden disappearance, and I was pleased at how quickly we resumed our usual dynamic. During our "catch-up session," as he'd called it (he was still reluctant to use the word "coaching"), he'd bragged that he was busier than ever, between dating a new woman he met on eHarmony and gearing up for his new movie—but the lack of feedback from his dalliance with Natasha had been gnawing at him. He'd asked whether I'd gotten any more specifics from her, and I was cagey. I'd told him she hadn't shared anything constructive, which was mostly true. I didn't want to betray her trust, and I figured in due time, Kent would bring up his premature declaration himself so I could address it more organically.

"She did say your interaction was passionate." I'd chosen the word deliberately, silently willing him to come clean. But perhaps he felt embarrassed after all this time, given that he didn't take the bait.

"That woman wouldn't know passion if it were grabbing her in the rain outside a rowboat in South Carolina!" Kent had sputtered. After recovering from his Ryan Gosling reference—*He'd seen* The Notebook*? What else didn't I know about him?*—I'd sighed, maybe a little too loudly. You could lead a horse to water, but the only beverage Kent seemed interested in drinking was his own Kool-Aid.

I redirected the conversation, inquiring about a woman he met online. "You hate that I met her on an app, don't you?" He'd chuckled, referencing what he viewed as my "competitor."

I'd let the comment slide, especially given my suggestion that he try online dating in the first place. He'd told me that the woman initially pushed for an upscale dinner for their first date, but that he heeded advice I'd given him previously and convinced her to try tapas instead. I was floored. Had Kent just acknowledged he followed my guidance? I knew he had before, based on some of his dates' feedback, but today was the first time he'd given me direct credit. (I didn't need it, but had to admit it felt nice.) I prefer drinks or tapas in lieu of formal dinners, at least for first dates, because it helps people get out of their heads.

In a formal dining scenario, people are more likely to assume their "Dating Personas"—a term I'd coined for identities people take on when they're nervous. When butterflies kick in, the rare breed can step up their game and turn on the charm, but the rest of us tend to show up as less desirable versions of ourselves. Anxiety may cause us to act restless or tense, and those muscular reactions trigger different behaviors or defense mechanisms to try to self-correct. Kent was a "Babbler," someone who talks way too much (in his case, often about himself) in front of someone else they find attractive. At a formal dinner where there are fewer distractions, this behavior can tank a date, but if your body can move and react to things around you—when strolling through a farmers market, visiting a museum, or experiencing multiple, natural interruptions of new plates during a tapas meal—conversation can flow more naturally.

Kent had shared what he'd learned about this new woman as a result. "She's into gardening, which I couldn't care less about." (I wanted to point out to him that gardening didn't seem all that removed from his love of harvesting grapes.) "But your ridiculous suggestion about acting like a talk show host worked. I asked who turned her on to gardening, what she's growing . . . I even asked if there's something else she'd enjoy cultivating in an alternate climate."

I'd felt a twinge of pride as he'd described putting my tips into practice. Curiosity may have killed the cat, but it usually saves the courtship. It must have been difficult for Kent to practice waiting for the Gardener to speak before chiming in with a story of his own, but by biting his tongue along with his patatas bravas, he made a connection with her—and learned fascinating tidbits by doing it.

"So how did you leave it with her?" I'd asked eagerly. "Is she going to give you a taste of one of her homegrown tomatoes?"

"As a matter of fact, yes. We're planning a second date for next weekend."

And there it was! A possible sign of growth!

"So," I'd continued, my interest piqued, "gardening aside, what do you like most about her?"

"Well, she was very Plain Jane at first, but she got prettier as we talked. She had this little twitch in her lips when she spoke. Maybe from nerves or regret from being there with me." (He then dismissed any possibility the latter could be true.) "It was cute. She also agreed the institution of marriage might be flawed. Or at least, she pretended to agree. But she point-blank asked if I own firearms. Which I do."

Despite this complication, his recap sounded mostly positive. I'd asked where he planned to take her next, and true to character, he protested the geography. (She lived in West Hollywood to his Eagle Rock. Like many LA residents, Kent typically allowed distance to play a major role in his dating life, despite having his own driver.) He'd then shared his intention to cook for her.

"So you're gonna make her drive all the way to you then?" I asked, trying my best to reserve judgment.

"I'm cooking, so it only seems fair."

I'd reminded him that it wasn't only about fairness, and wondered whether the drive was some sort of test he was posing to her. (After all, he could just send a car to pick her up, as I'd known him to do before.)

"No," Kent had answered, visibly irritated. "Why would you ask that?"

I'd given him a knowing look. "Maybe if she drives to you, it will demonstrate she's willing to do her fair share of the commuting in the relationship," I'd theorized. "Or, maybe if she's *too* willing, it will subconsciously turn you off."

"Why would it do that?"

"Because you're looking for someone confident—someone who doesn't feel the need to make herself overly available to you. Maybe if she drives to you this early, you'll wind up writing her off as overly eager."

"That's stupid." His eyes had twinkled. "How well you know me, I mean."

"Let's not test the Gardener so soon then," I'd recommended, trying to stifle a smile. "I like her for you."

I meant it, but was he going to step up his game with her, or resort to making up excuses once something "inconvenient" arose—an inevitably in any long-term relationship? Kent was a successful, good-looking guy who was also playful and intelligent. But he was also cocky, stubborn, and impatient. To ultimately connect with her, he was going to have to get in touch with his more modest, sensitive, and tolerant side—something I was finally starting to notice.

"Oh, and Kent?" I asked, before logging out.

"Yes?" He'd raised his eyebrows, as if he knew what was coming.

"No more disappearing on me, okay? I'm in it for the long haul."

The weekend away was exactly what I needed. I felt restored, both in my connection with Dave and in our continued commitment to expand our family. We also decided to switch IVF clinics. I had been willing to give our doctor a second chance, but she provided little hope or comfort that she intended to approach our case any differently moving forward. If a client's needs weren't getting met in a relationship, they expressed that to their partner, and their partner had no intention to address it, I would encourage them to leave that relationship. Ultimately, I realized I shouldn't hold our fertility doctor to a lesser standard.

The idea of starting from scratch elsewhere felt scary, but the unknown had to be better than the constant anxiety and disappointment I would inevitably feel by not taking action. The new plan gave me hope, and sometimes that's all that's needed to change the course of your life for the better.

THE INNER MONOLOGUE

For most of the trip, I was able to relax and enjoy reconnecting with Dave. I relished the time away from the city, and having a clean bathroom devoid of medicine, needles, and gauze pads. For the first time in a while, I also hadn't felt preoccupied with client-related logistics, as Lauren had kindly offered to "take over" during my vacation. It was nice to prioritize my own love life without having to simultaneously juggle everyone else's.

But as Dave drove home, true to form, I found myself immediately wondering how my clients' dates went that weekend. I refreshed my inbox curiously, but no updates had come through yet. So instead, I closed my eyes and allowed my mind to wander. The change I had seen in Kent this last session, however slight, was motivating. It was a good reminder that even when I don't notice immediate progress with someone, it doesn't necessarily mean my advice isn't resonating with them—as evidenced by his willingness to tackle his "Dating Persona" on his last date. Once clients start doing this, I usually see significant change in their dating habits and results.

Some nervous dating habits could be indicators of larger issues (e.g., not giving the other person a chance to speak might suggest narcissism, or shutting down a bit might signal social unease), but I don't believe most daters are manipulative or undesirable candidates for partnership. While that's important to ascertain, so is whether or not someone is well suited for you: something that can be easily missed if your date's behavior is affected by nerves. Conversely, you don't want your date misinterpreting your character or intentions either.

So what are the most common nervous dating habits, along with their accompanying personas, and how can we best combat them to achieve our desired result? In addition to "Babblers" such as Kent, I regularly encounter "Bares," "Clams," "Stiffs," "Workaholics," and "Self-Sabotagers."

Everyone loves talking about themselves, but for a Babbler, monologuing is a crutch. They typically feel pressure to fill silences, whether that's by trying to make someone laugh or impress them. (A subcategory of Babblers, aka Boasters—name-droppers and braggarts compelled to tell you what important people they know, or how spectacular they are—are motivated by the latter. A Jewish client of mine, referring to a doctor applauding himself on their date for all his charitable works, told me she was turned off by him "competing in the Mensch Olympics." This nervous dating habit is occasionally driven by insecurity—after all, if you were confident in what you had to offer, you might be inclined to show it rather than tell it.) Silence can be an opportunity to regroup or even connect with someone nonverbally, but unfortunately, Babblers deprive themselves of those experiences.

If you're a Babbler, try waiting for your date to speak first occasionally. If they don't, and the silence is too much to bear, sip a drink or even excuse yourself to the restroom. You should also ask more questions to allow your date to do more of the talking. This demonstrates that you are present, and that you care. (Otherwise your date might go home feeling as if they learned so much about you, but that you had little interest in getting to know them.)

If you're unsure what to ask, pretend you have to write an essay on one of your date's hobbies or interests, and your date is your only source. If they enjoy diving for scallops, for example, ask who turned them on to it. Did they go on any expeditions recently? Do they usually do this activity alone, or with a friend? *The Book of Beautiful Questions: The Powerful Questions That Will Help You Decide, Create, Connect, and Lead* by the "questionologist" Warren Berger offers some thought-provoking questions, not only to help improve your interpersonal communications, but also to improve your relationship with yourself. (I recommended it to Kent, who replied: *"You think I have time to read, Jaydi?"*) The psychologist Arthur Aron also has a fantastic list of thirty-six questions designed to lead two people toward a more intimate relationship, something he created following a 1997 study he conducted at the State University of New York at Stony Brook. I've tested it firsthand and can assure you: it works!

If you're on a date with a Babbler, I recommend playfully pointing out their behavior to them. A former client, and dating expert in her own right, Gabi Conti, did this skillfully on her first date with her husband. After barely coming up for air the first hour, he asked her if she wanted another drink with him. Her reply? "I will only have another drink if you start asking me questions about myself." Unaware how he'd been coming off until then, he quickly apologized, and the tone of the date shifted completely. It turned out he'd been having an off day, and appreciated her candor. (If his response had been rude, Gabi would have moved on to someone new. And she wouldn't have minded either, since her now-husband was coming off as too self-indulgent anyway!)

When clients shoot down second dates with Babblers who are otherwise amazing catches, I'm disappointed. After all, if someone is chatty on their date, it's usually a sign they're excited and having fun with you. If you can overlook their nervous tendency to ramble, they can truly make great partners (I would know: Dave is one!). Babblers are usually outgoing and have interesting stories to share that will entertain you for years to come. If you're someone like me who enjoys a mental break from time to time, allowing someone else to take the lead in conversation can be relaxing. It's also worth noting that a Babbler might also be eloquent in other situations, such as at work. For these reasons, and many more, I usually push my clients to grant second dates to Babblers if everything else feels in alignment.

Another Dating Persona to look out for is the "Soul Barer," or "Bare" (not to be confused with the gay subculture "Bears"). While Babblers talk too much, Bares *share* too much. When opening up, they mistake their feeling of vulnerability for actually forming a connection with someone ("I felt comfortable baring my soul to them; therefore they must be my soulmate"). As a result, they have a tendency to engage in longer dates, which on the surface might feel exciting ("surely our date is going well if this person wants to be here with me this long") but is ultimately not the best indicator of potential.

As a result of oversharing, a Bare can also give the impression that their lives are full of hardship. Naturally, if you had a traumatic sexual encounter when you were younger or your dad was recently diagnosed with cancer, you'll likely want a partner who can eventually help shoulder the weight of those burdens. But you want your date to learn about you, not just what's happened to you. If you can't let loose for a couple of hours, and withhold more personal information until date two or three, you might inadvertently give off the impression you have trouble having fun. When describing their ideal partner, the two most common traits straight men usually request are positivity and lighter energy. There's a reason people refer to that giddy, post-date feeling as "floating." Most people want to end up with someone whose life appears generally happy. Heavy topics such as health issues, exes, and prior trauma might indicate otherwise. This doesn't mean you should change everything about your personality if you're naturally more serious or lead with your intellect, but everyone has some kind of baggage. (Some people's just weighs less than others' or accompanies them on private jets.) Before someone knows whether they want to take on yours, they need to know how they feel about *you*. So, who are you? It's a simple question with a very complex answer. But unless you know, your date can't be expected to, either.

If you're out with a Bare, you *bear* some responsibility to guide the tone and pace for the first date and beyond. Keep the initial meetup light, and don't exceed more than two hours with someone. In fact, if you get the sense you're on a date with a Bare, give them a polite heads-up that, while you're happy to be there with them, you have a hard out. This should help them keep their vulnerability in check. If necessary, you can also redirect the conversation. If talking about the death of a Bare's father is sending them down a rabbit hole, consider asking where their dad is from or what his favorite movie was. That person will likely feel relief moving on to a slightly lighter subject. This only applies to the early stages of dating, though.

I'm not suggesting anyone be an insensitive dummy! If redirecting the conversation isn't working, they might be oversharing as a way to push your relationship with them forward, all while avoiding real vulnerability: behavior that research professor, author, and motivational speaker Brené Brown describes as "floodlighting." If your date insists on treating your time together as a therapy session, this is probably a character flaw rather than a nervous dating habit.

Being with a genuine Bare has benefits, though. Oftentimes they've been through difficult situations—ones they can't help but divulge to you. And being with someone who's experienced hardship can be comforting. If you have too, you might experience an emotional connection more easily with them. If you haven't, you might feel safer knowing you're with someone who weathered a storm, and hopefully emerged the better and stronger for it. They're also potentially someone who won't run away during conflict. And if they were vulnerable enough to share their experiences with you, this likely means you'll have a partner who will always be truthful down the road—if anything, to a fault. If you suspect you went out with a Bare, try an activity for your second date. It's a great way to organically get to know each other without the pressure of heavy conversation. By the third date, if they're looking to open up to you more, I'd not only encourage that, but also plan to do the same in return.

Next, some people don't talk too much or say too much on a date: instead, they say too little. I call those who shut down when nervous "Clams." Daters like Meera can be confident as all hell at work, but face-to-face with someone they like, a different personality emerges. Surprisingly, many of my on-camera clients (actors, hosts, broadcast journalists, etc.), who are extremely comfortable performing publicly, often have trouble "turning on" that version of themselves on dates. Even when asked a question, sometimes all they can manage is nervous laughter. This shyness is exactly why Clams like Meera should avoid Bares. After all, what better opportunity for a Bare to work their magic than hours of conversation with someone who often forgets to speak?

I've discovered tricks for Clams to open themselves up, though, and I've worked on some of them with Meera. Before a date, ask yourself: what do you love most about who you are that you'd want a potential love interest to learn too? (This question also helps with constructing online dating profiles.) I have a client who's Ivy League educated with her MBA. She's a master at Octordle, a trivia night champion, part Venezuelan, and she holds three citizenships. She also has a beautiful smile and lights up when any of those topics come up. But if she shuts down and doesn't discuss any of it, I'm not sure why *anyone* would want a second date with her. So, for Clams, going into the date knowing exactly what you'd like the other person to learn about you can help. Changing locations is useful too—even if that means taking a bathroom break to regroup. Alternatively, if you and your date have finished your appetizers and entrées, you can propose to skip dessert and grab ice cream a few blocks away instead. Not only will your spontaneity likely be appreciated, but you'll also get your blood flowing again—maybe just enough to get your tongue flowing too (in more ways than one)!

If you're on a date with a possible Clam, it's helpful to remember that just because they're shy with you, it doesn't mean they aren't outgoing with friends or family. So how can you tell? Patience is key. Allow lulls in the conversation to see whether they're willing to initiate. And try to be encouraging so they don't feel judged (because yes, they're likely aware they're being too quiet and desperately racking their brain for the best thing to say next). Clams can have a hard time talking about themselves initially, but they're usually okay speaking about other subjects. *Was there a lot of traffic coming here? How 'bout those Mets?* If all else fails, teasing will usually do the trick: *Are you always this quiet? I'm guessing from your silence you must really like me, huh?* The teasing, as long as it's playful, will show you're interested in—and not turned off by—their behavior. Clams are often living in their own heads, so getting them to crack a smile will always help make them more present.

A Clam might actually be socially awkward, or introverted, but in either case remember: just because they're more reserved than you doesn't mean they aren't worth knowing. Some Clams are the most interesting people in the world, and can make really ideal partners.

Then there's others like me: "Stiffs." Before my Confident Era, just before I met Dave, I would act really formal on first dates, and men found me hard to read. Unlike Babblers or Clams, Stiffs' defense mechanisms have nothing to do with how much or how little we say: it's how we *move*. We sit up straight, sip our drinks, and adopt a general attitude of "formal is normal." What is *not* normal, however, is for our dates to feel like our connection with them has potential.

Stiffs can also appear intimidating. The more interested in you we are, the more formal we might act, and the more formal we act, the less interested in you we may seem. What we do have in common with all the other Dating Personas, though, is that our behavior jeopardizes our chances of getting another date with someone. In the past, if I was lucky enough to get a second, I'd usually relax more at that point, and it was "game on." Like other Stiffs, I can be playful, warm, and generally delightful once that side of me is coaxed out (and I think I'm worth the effort!). But had I been able to unleash that side of myself when I was younger, on my own—well, my prospects would have grown exponentially.

The pandemic actually helped me recognize and address my

Stiff behavior. Conducting countless intake interviews and coaching sessions on Zoom forced me to see myself more often, and it was easy to see why others had claimed I'd been hard to read. I had a very clear "resting bitch face" (RBF—a misogynistic term for the unpleasant, and usually unconscious, expression one might have when not feeling a particular emotion at all). My RBF had been pointed out to me before, in jest, so it was something I was aware of. But encountering it head-on made me realize it was time to make a change. Through conducting Zoom sessions in "gallery mode," a feature that allows you to see yourself along with other participants on-screen, I started working on my expressions more. What felt like a wide, forced grin at times was really only the corners of my lips slightly turned up.

Making that feel natural would take time, but fortunately, facial expressions can be learned through a combination of observation and practice. Over time, and with enough attention to it, people started perceiving me to be generally happier and more welcoming. My outsides were finally matching my insides! Because that strategy worked for me, I started prescribing Zoom dates as practice to my Stiff clients. By seeing themselves on dates, and learning how to adjust their facial muscles and posture, they could actually train their bodies to respond as they hoped them to in situations with higher stakes. (And potentially save themselves years of Botox in the process!)

For Stiffs, it's also important for us to know what makes us smile widely. Maybe we love talking about our nephew or last vacation to Mexico, or maybe it's the latest episode of *Love Island*. Either way, it's important to identify what those subjects are, and make a point of bringing them up to potential partners. Expressing passion isn't the same as exuding warmth, but it does elicit similar energy—energy most people find attractive.

Lastly, while clothing choice can affect everyone positively, it's integral for Stiffs. When I'm cold, for example, I'm much more likely to act uptight. Most people associate sweating with nerves, but cold sensations are even more common for people with anxiety. If I dress warmly in jeans and a sweater, I'm ten times more likely to feel at ease in my environment. This doesn't mean you shouldn't dress your best (if you're a Stiff and you're convinced you're going to impress more by strutting into a restaurant in a minidress and heels in the winter, at least bring a jacket to throw on after that first impression is made). Ultimately, though, I advise Stiff clients to wear what makes them feel like *them*. After all, it won't matter that they're showing off their boobs if they're being a complete boob on the date.

Should you ever find yourself on a date with a Stiff, I implore you—don't assume we aren't interested in you. Look for clues that a Stiff might actually be engaged on your date. Are they asking you questions? How's their eye contact? Are they leaving the date early, or are they staying to talk to you more? What happens if you go on a walk with them? Does their body language or intonation change once they're in motion? Stiffs, once comfortable, are often the most affectionate daters of all. But you'll never get to see that side of us if you write us off as disinterested.

"Workaholics" are another Dating Persona I encounter regularly. These business professionals and creatives have trouble getting out of "work mode." Without realizing it, the majority of all their stories and references on dates wind up circling back to their jobs, and in worst-case scenarios, they even check work emails on the date itself, unable to "turn it off." An Oscar-winning director client of mine was often guilty of this. He'd write to me afterward that he wanted to see his dates again, but the women he went out with were regularly shocked to hear that feedback. "He left after forty-five minutes," one complained, "and he was on his phone the entire time. He told you he *liked* me?!"

Dates with Workaholics can feel rushed and demoralizing. While these men or women might be impressive, if they can't even prioritize a date for a couple of hours, one might wonder how they could possibly maintain a healthy relationship. Everyone wants a partner they can admire, and some people are specifically looking to be one half of a "power couple." But most singles I work with are more likely to admire their eventual partner because of that person's kindness, self-assuredness, or love of family rather than for what they do for a living (provided there is stability, passion, and drive behind it). If you're a Workaholic, you don't need to tone down your accomplishments or aspirations. But just as hardships don't define Bares, successess don't define Workaholics.

So, what can you do to get out of work mode? First, try to avoid scheduling first dates after work. If you're not stressing about your job all day, you're much less likely to bring that energy to a date. If you have to go on a date from work, at least change your clothes first. Like Stiffs, Workaholics can be strongly affected by what they wear. An agent I work with is known to show up to a casual date in a suit worn to work that day. And an on-set teacher I coach was guilty of not changing into something more date-appropriate prior to going out. No matter how much she tried leaving work life behind her, shifting from educating a two-year-old to flirting with a thirty-two-year-old was all the more difficult when she had spit-up on her shirt. If you're a Workaholic, take advantage of the walk or the drive to your date spot. Can you queue up a Chappell Roan song or favorite crime podcast that makes you forget about your boss you want to kill? Listen to that as you leave work, and whatever you do, don't check those outstanding emails after pulling into the parking lot.

If you're on a date with a Workaholic, it's hard not to feel somewhat offended that they aren't solely focused on you. But this distraction doesn't make them a bad partner—it simply means they might need a little help unwinding. If you end up being the person who can do that for them, by sharing a drink or making them laugh, you might just find a very special person on the other side. The director I mentioned is a gregarious natural leader who unwinds on the most epic of ski vacations. He's now a wonderful father to his newborn son, a proud homeowner, and a great listener once he learned how to put down his phone.

Last is the only persona you want to avoid entirely: "Self-Sabotagers." They ruin dates before realizing their potential, and are guilty of rejecting others before they can be rejected themselves (think those who swipe right on dating app profiles, only to lose interest the moment that person matches with them back). They also have a tendency to interrogate their dates: *Are you over your ex? How many kids do you want? When do you want them by? Do you get along with your family?* If someone winds up passing their test, it might already be too late: that person is too turned off by *them*.

Self-Sabotagers also rarely enter into relationships, because their search parameters are too rigid or based on absurd premises. A client once told me she wanted an unusual-looking partner: "The uglier the better. I want all eyes focused on *me* when I walk into a room." A TV writer acquaintance "knows" that his future wife also works in the entertainment industry and isn't open to introductions outside of that. One podcaster shared that her ideal type is "Cluster Bs," referencing men with certain personality disorders. And I even coached a guy obsessed with dating sims, a video game subgenre popular in Japan, who was too shy to attempt actual dating. (I've toyed with prescribing dating simulators as "homework" for certain personality types, as some are very well written and have actionable, positive takeaways.)

If a Self-Sabotager does get into a relationship, the complications don't necessarily stop there, as their unchecked patterns are bound to repeat themselves. Unfortunately, the only predictable future for Self-Sabotagers is that they will likely remain single—at least without doing proper work on themselves. Coaches and therapists can help with that, but you should probably wait to date that person until they're in a better headspace. I have a soft spot for Self-Sabotager clients like Callie, because they clearly want to be in relationships (otherwise, why bother paying for matchmaking or date coaching?) but often don't realize how they're getting in their own way.

I felt I was finally starting to get through to Callie, and was confident I could help her in time. But with her self-imposed ticking clock, I worried: would there be enough of it left?

Callie was responding well to my new tough-love approach, but she was progressing slowly. While she'd finally stopped resisting the matches I curated, once in front of them, she continued to act more like their interviewer than a possible love interest. In one case, she was even borderline rude, making her disinterest to them clear.

"You've got it all," I bemoaned to her. "You're confident and can flirt like nobody's business, but you're grilling people like they're your meal instead of your actual date, and you're still not getting to know them—at least not in a real way."

I brought up exit surveys I conduct with clients whenever they meet their significant others outside our service. Roughly half the time, clients wind up with someone who checks off all their major boxes. The other times, noticeable "asks" are missing—yet both sets appeared equally happy in their relationships. That's because long-term happiness with a partner is not predicated on having all preferences met. It's about avoiding the dealbreakers.

"I could only introduce you to men and women who check off all your boxes," I attempted to placate her, "but that doesn't mean you'll have chemistry with them." No one was trying to sacrifice quality here. "Shorter men, older women, women carrying extra weight, divorcées with kids, men with receding hairlines . . . all of these outliers have an equal shot at making you blissfully happy," I emphasized, "if all the other components are in place."

Callie nodded, sharing that she'd always told her friends that divorced people make the best partners. "At least you know they can commit!"

Daters in some outlier categories also tend to excel in other areas. For example, single moms tend to be more nurturing. Men who aren't as tall tend to be more charismatic or display higher intelligence (because they aren't able to rely on their height to get by—take short kings Tom Holland, Dave Franco, and Kevin Hart, for example). Callie reminded me that she had to be attracted to the person she was going to spend the rest of her life with. I agreed, but added that she might be surprised by whom she could be attracted to. Right now, Callie still seemed very set in her ways, and she was going to have to be much more open-minded if she was going to find her forever partner. As it stood, she had merely graduated from writing people off *before* meeting them to writing them off afterward.

To drive home the point, I asked her to think back to a recent Hinge date she rejected. He was a traditionally attractive lawyer who likely could have given her a run for her money on the pickleball court, but she'd been overly distressed by his enthusiasm for aquariums. It was a rarefied interest she didn't think that she could connect to, and so she had blanketly decided there was no future with him.

"You have to admit it's a weird hobby," she said as we analyzed her decision to cut him loose.

"It's unusual," I acknowledged. "But if you had established more of an emotional connection with him, I bet you wouldn't have cared if he was"—I paused to look back at her email about him, wanting to quote her words exactly—"'too into freshwater fish.' You're still looking for reasons to rule people out instead of ruling them in."

I told her I wanted her to leave room for someone to surprise her or teach her something new. I also insisted she remain present and engaged, even if she was leaning toward not seeing someone again. They still took time out of their evening to be with her. Dismissing someone so quickly not only sends a message that you aren't interested in another date with them; it also conveys disrespect, implies they have nothing valuable to share, and sends the message you're devaluing them as a person.

"Maybe their roommate is a perfect match for you," I appealed to her more selfish instincts, in case being viewed as kind wasn't enough incentive. "There's no way they'd ever suggest an intro, though, if you were rude."

Callie cocked her head and nodded, acknowledging my point. She explained that she hadn't wanted to waste anyone's time, or lead them on, if she didn't see a connection going somewhere, but admitted she never considered how her behavior might be perceived or internalized by another.

She assured me she'd try harder moving forward to get to know her dates better, if only for their potentially cute roommate.

THE HOLLYWOOD MONTAGE

Cuffing season was upon us, and good news started pouring in from clients. Aside from a few recent pairings going well, word on the street was that Don and Evie, a couple I'd introduced a couple of years back, were talking about taking "next steps" in their relationship. Don, a PR exec, had stood out initially, because he'd insisted he was drawn toward a more "homely" look (it's not a descriptor we often hear). But after introducing him to Evie, we realized he wasn't looking for someone "homely" at all, but rather someone who felt like home.

I wondered what their "next steps" would be. Would he and Evie move in together—or fulfill every matchmaker's ultimate dream by getting engaged? When it comes to successful outcomes in a relationship, there's no right "order" to things. I've seen couples get engaged after only dating a few months, have babies before getting married, and move in together before getting engaged—and those people are still together, and happy, decades later. But I do believe holding firm to your preference, whatever that might be, can speed up an eventual outcome.

My very traditional mother always taught me that a man is less likely to "buy the milk" when he can "get the cow for free." (I prefer to think of moving in together as an "expensive fur coat" and the woman as an "elegant snow leopard," but why argue over semantics?) Not wanting to chance her being right, I clung to my West Hollywood apartment before Dave and I got engaged—a move he saw as a "waste of money," and a mere technicality since I was sleeping at his condo on the other side of town nearly every night.

"You can't really know someone unless you live with them first," he said, echoing a sentiment I'd heard dozens of friends and clients express before him. And to help convince me of this logic, he'd made every effort to make his place feel like "ours." He made room for my clothes in his closet, helped assemble a cabinet for my toiletries, and even let me replace his beloved mid-century modern sofa—an affront to my preference for a more bohemian aesthetic.

To some extent, he was right that moving in together could help us learn more about our general compatibility—how else would I have discovered that he went to bed early to wake up at an ungodly hour the next day to work out? And how else would he have learned about my disinterest in making the bed—a slothful move he categorized as "barbaric"?

Still, I'm not convinced that learning those things before an engagement or marriage would have made a difference—after all, those lifestyle choices might be inconvenient for the other, but neither would come close to outweighing the reasons we chose to be together. Our hybrid living dynamic suited us, though. It allowed us to spend more time together while preserving my feeling of safety. Keeping my apartment, even in name only, was what I needed to feel confident and comfortable, but what worked for me might not for someone else. I wondered what Evie and Don would need to feel confident and comfortable. I hoped that whatever that was, they were both on the same page about it.

In addition to Evie and Don's exciting but nebulous update, more positive ones followed. An Emmy-winning writer, a popular TikTok influencer, and the real-life subject of a Netflix anthology series all activated memberships the same week, as did a celebrity assistant. I soon realized the latter had dated one of my ex-boyfriends, and she'd only learned at the end of their brief relationship that she was his "side piece." He was married with a kid now, but had misled her into believing he and his wife had been separated at the time. *Still a schmuck*, she confirmed to me when we met.

"I'm so sorry," I empathized, imagining what might have happened if he and I had stayed together. "Did you tell his wife?"

"No." She wavered. "Should I have?"

I wasn't sure how to answer. I'd never met his wife, but from all accounts, she sounded sweet, intelligent, and accomplished. Aside from her weakness of choosing the wrong men, my new client seemed like a catch too. (At least our mutual ex had taste.)

I also had a string of sign-ups who were disgruntled former clients of various industry giants. One of them, Kathy, was fifty-one, five-foot-eight, and a statuesque blonde with a bank account the size of her appetite in men. I admit, I was surprised that after just dropping a hundred thousand dollars at a matchmaking company that didn't live up to her expectations, she was more than willing to try mine (but I was glad she was). She ranted about her past experience, which included signing a nondisparagement clause after receiving a partial refund—a common practice at some of these larger companies. (Going to great lengths to maintain a favorable public image is not unusual. Many owners hire firms who specialize in online-reputation management.)

I considered how to help her. A confident and intelligent strategic consultant, Kathy also had a cheeky personality. "The only green things I love are money and emeralds," she'd told me when I asked how outdoorsy she was. She'd also insisted she didn't want to be a "nurse or a purse" when specifying her desired age range. At first blush, she appeared to be a "catch," and my guess was that the other company's database simply didn't support the type of men she was seeking. (Kathy had mostly been presented with struggling actors and musicians, some of whom didn't even live in-state, which was the total antithesis of the private-island-owning, local venture capitalists "sold" to her during her initial consultation.) What's more, her matchmaker had defended the matches, insisting they were "first-rate" because they were "hot" or "owned property"—no reasoning as to why they were particularly well suited for her. *Some of these business owners,* I thought, *should be selling cars—not matchmaking.* If our industry had even more regulation, perhaps they would be.

Years ago, matchmaker and businesswoman Lisa Clampitt noticed the lack of continuing education, certification process, and strong community for modern-day love connectors, and founded the much-needed Global Love Institute (formerly known as the Matchmaking Institute) in 2003. Through her courses, over two thousand matchmakers and relationship experts from more than twenty-five countries—including yours truly—have become certified. She also initiated the world's first global love conferences. What Lisa has done for our community is tremendous, including her twelve-week curriculum and optional courses, exposure to collaboration opportunities, and offer to serve as mediator during professional conflicts. But there's more work to be done.

Being entrusted to help someone on their journey to find love is a huge responsibility, and can be closely linked to a client's mental health. Therefore, a governing body for our industry should not only include an ethics code that our members must abide by, but also consequences should we break it—akin to what the American Psychological Association, the American Association for Marriage and Family Therapy, and the American Counseling Association demand. While the bar of entry is higher for those associations, and should be, more pillars should be in place to help protect our clients. As it stands, they have little to no recourse if they feel harmed, or taken advantage of, by services rendered. In our industry, some customer dissatisfaction is unavoidable—it's virtually impossible to "get it right" for everyone during a process that's so subjective. But some companies sacrifice outcome for profit, whether it's out of greed or ignorance, and those shortcuts can be damaging.

As I conducted a deeper dive on Kathy's preferences, one in particular concerned me. Under no circumstances did she want to meet any Asian men. This was a sensitive subject, as I view parameters like that as inherently racist—after all, no one race or ethnicity is a monolith, and she couldn't possibly know her capacity to be attracted to someone she's never met before. I was careful to express curiosity rather than judgment, though. After all, when I first started matchmaking, I used to ask for clients' preferences on race or ethnicity in my intake interview—the same way I'd ask their political and religious beliefs.

But a Facebook post by a colleague, Carmelia Ray, challenged my views on that. "Is it racist if someone excludes a particular race in their dating preferences?" she posed to the group we were in at large. The responses were widely divided. Some felt it was our job to honor all clients' preferences, and likened the situation to someone expressing a preference for blondes or brunettes. Preferences are different from dealbreakers, though. Unlike religion or politics, race itself is rarely tied to a difference in values, and alone shouldn't prevent two people from connecting. Similarly, I would think it absurd if someone categorically ruled out a potential husband or wife over their hair color.

After much reflection, I landed on eliminating the race-based question I had on my intake interview, replacing it with: "Have you ever dated outside your race or ethnicity?" The question wasn't suggesting whether someone should or shouldn't. Instead, the answer would offer valuable insight into a prospective client's dating practices, and just how open they really were. Some people have responded with a straightforward "yes" or "no" while others have elaborated, sharing that although they historically hadn't dated outside their own race, they were more than open to doing so. Others have taken the opportunity to share which races they were opposed to meeting romantically, or shared even more specific requests such as favoring light-skinned people over dark-skinned people (a racist practice known as colorism).

Many of these people don't view their preferences as racist, and I am not looking to label them. But I actively want to work with clients who are able to recognize their shortcomings, and have a desire to correct them, as they are certain to be holding these daters back. Most of the time, someone's implicit bias stems from a lack of exposure to a particular group of people (explaining why I saw an uptick of women interested in Asian men after the release of the movie *Crazy Rich Asians*), and when appropriate, I'm glad to give them some.

Kathy is white, but I've also worked with many *minority* clients who have preferences about dating within their own race—and in those cases, I try to honor that. I can't possibly know the negative experiences and challenges someone has faced as a member of a particular minority group, and it might help them feel more connected emotionally to a partner who can relate. When the opposite happens, such as when Meera claimed other South Asians reminded her too much of family, I try to get them to reconsider if the match I have in mind is strong enough. (If I'd honored my husband's preference to avoid all Jewish women, we wouldn't be together!)

While I don't fashion myself the arbiter of romantic racism, when it comes to matchmaking, I do try to remove race from the equation whenever possible, and shared that with Kathy. She heard me, and reassured me she would remain open if I ever had a match in mind who differed from what she currently envisioned for herself. "After all, you're the expert," she conceded. I could tell she was going to be a challenging client, but for now, her deference on the subject was enough.

That week, I was also delighted to be setting up a local gay matchmaker who didn't want to dip into his own client pool. Some matchmaking companies won't work with LGBTQ+ singles—they don't have enough database members to offer them—but I'd been determined to build out a dating pool that could cater to them too. Doing so had taken time, but it was a really rewarding and worthwhile investment.

It had also been deeply educational. Early on, when I'd made it a point to accept any quality referral, I was frustrated by the lack of success I was having in the LGBTQ+ community. It took a straightforward conversation with my husband's single friend Adam, during his intake interview, to realize what the problem was. "I mean for me, and nothing against these types of people," he started, sounding a bit self-conscious, "but I'm not really into bears, or more effeminate folks, and nothing wrong with bald or salt-and-pepper hair, but they aren't really my type. And absolutely no name-droppers or anyone who wears tank tops," he told me after I inquired about his dealbreakers. "Oh, and no one who shaves their body or posts thirst-trap selfies."

I nodded, frantically writing all of this down.

"I'm a top, by the way. You normally ask your clients that, right?"

"Should I?" I leaned in curiously. I'd never asked my straight clients about their sexual habits before, unless they volunteered to share (most do if they're into BDSM or kink, or if they lack experience entirely).

"Yes!" He laughed as if stating the obvious. "They'll feel safer with you, like you actually know what you're talking about."

"Really?" I was skeptical.

"Trust me." And he was right. Until then, I'd been conducting intake interviews with queer clients the same way I was for my cisgender, straight singles, which didn't inspire much confidence. The relief on my colleague's face when I asked him about sexual preferences—among other subtler, more thoughtful questions about his lifestyle and taste—confirmed this.

While a goal was to monetize the LGBTQ+ portion of my membership, once I had the database to support it, the larger goal was—and will continue to be—to set up as many successful couples as possible. When scrolling through the "Success Stories" section of my website, I want the page to reflect the diversity of all the clients I work with. I wasn't sure what kind of child I was going to bring into the world one day, but knew that I would want them to feel accepted, and supported by, a company like mine, regardless of their background.

THE LIGHT BULB MOMENT

Around the time that another round of my eggs were getting fertilized at the new IVF clinic, Meera was at home punishing herself for putting all of hers in one basket. For the last few weeks, Trevor had dangled the arrival of his mother, who was planning to visit from Nebraska, and promised that the two would meet. An introduction to her would be a big step, as Meera saw it, one that had convinced her things with Trevor were headed in the right direction. Until they weren't.

The day of the planned meetup, just after Meera had left work early to get a fresh blowout, Trevor texted her that he wasn't feeling well. "I think we're just gonna hang in tonight instead. Sorry, babe," he added, with a frown face emoji. "I'll find a way to make it up to you." Only, he couldn't. Trevor's mom was only in town for the weekend, and no romantic dinner or gesture the following one would be an adequate substitute for what Meera deemed the metaphorical representation of Trevor's love: an introduction to the most important woman in his life.

She didn't wait long before booking a session with me. She was considering ending things with Trevor this time, and knew if she delayed acting on her hurt and frustration any longer, he'd find a way to gaslight her into believing their relationship still had potential. But now she wasn't so sure she wanted to be convinced.

A person on the receiving end of a breakup can react in one of two ways: they can break, or they can break away. "I'll spread my wings and I'll learn how to fly," Kelly Clarkson wrote in her power ballad "Breakaway," about leaving her hometown in order to pursue her music career. A fresh start can feel daunting, even insurmountable, but the reward at the end can be more than worth it. In Meera's case, though, would mourning another failed relationship set her back? Or would this experience finally be what gave her wings to chase the kind of relationship she ultimately deserved?

She implored me when we met up that afternoon to share all the negative things I wanted to say about Trevor but didn't, because I'd been worried about sparing her feelings. I had plenty I could share but needed to tread lightly. If I said anything too harsh, only for those two to later get back together—a likely outcome if I were to go by her dating history—our coaching relationship could be compromised. So instead, I went with: "It's becoming pretty clear he isn't ready for a relationship." It was an observation rather than a dig at his character. "He's exactly who he's been telling you he is—other than your intense second date with him, which was nearly six months ago at this point. You just haven't been listening." But she was listening now, so I continued. I told her that I didn't think he was a malicious guy or stringing her along on purpose. Trevor, in all likelihood, was merely lost. And he was never going to figure out a future with Meera if he was still discovering what he wanted on his own. "I know it's easier to hate him for that, but he's probably dealing with his own baggage that he hasn't sorted through yet, and is filtering everything through that lens. His canceling dinner probably had nothing to do with you—maybe he really was sick, or his mom wasn't interested in meeting you, and he was embarrassed to say that."

"Do you think that's it?" She perked up. I should have known better than to make possible excuses for him.

I told her the reason wasn't important. What was worth examining, however, was his inability to communicate that to her. He wasn't thinking about how his actions impacted her, which is what anyone should want from a potential life partner.

"So you're saying he's selfish." She raised her eyebrows.

"I'm saying he's *acting* selfishly," I corrected her. "And you deserve a guy who's going to be more attuned to your emotional needs. Regularly. Someone who recognizes the impact of their actions on other people. You want Trevor to change, and maybe he will one day: with lots of therapy, a great deal of self-awareness, and a desire to grow. But you can't give him that. He has to want that for himself. And I'm not sure that's a priority for him right now."

I wasn't sure whether Meera had ever read *He's Just Not That into You* or seen the film adaptation of it starring Ginnifer Goodwin. Either way, she wasn't alone in believing that she could be the motivating factor for someone to change their fundamental nature. Like Ginnifer's character in the movie, Meera believed she might be a man's "exception." But who wants to bank their twenties or thirties on being someone else's exception? Wouldn't you rather someone else be yours?

To capitalize on Meera's seeming willingness to move on, I threw out an exercise. I referenced our previous coaching session on red flags and asked her to verbalize Trevor's. It was encouraging to hear her call him "intense" and "controlling," and I was glad to hear her point out his inconsistent behavior, which had been the focus of our recent conversations. Still, she seemed unsure this was enough cause to give up on his potential.

"Everyone has red flags, don't they?" she asked almost hopefully.

I cocked my head in partial agreement. Nobody is or could be perfect, and everyone has flaws they can work on. But some behaviors in the romantic sphere are more concerning than others, and once they're pointed out, that person needs to be receptive to changing them. So far, though, Trevor hadn't offered anything beyond empty promises.

I also reminded her that breaking up with him was pointless if she was unwilling to address her own major red flag—something she jokingly alluded to in an earlier session—allowing someone to continue to treat her poorly without consequence. "Now don't start thinking you're perfect for each other, because you both have things you need to work on," I said comically, wondering whether I actually might have read her mind. "Sometimes these journeys are best made separately."

Meera agreed, and to my great shock and comfort, she shared she was going to break up with Trevor later that night. At last we could focus on her healing, something that would provide so much comfort—to herself, and also to the special someone she hadn't yet met.

"You seem happy," Kent commented during a session later that month. He was now firmly in the habit of commenting on my perceived emotional state every time we met. And once again, he wasn't wrong.

Dave and I had recently learned that our IVF round at the new clinic resulted in three healthy embryos. "I guess I am happy," I offered, figuring if I accepted his observation, rather than protest it, it would be easier to move on. I asked whether he was feeling the same. He said he felt "vindicated," which to him was close enough. He'd recently ended things with the Gardener and doubled down on not wanting to date women who live outside a five-mile radius from him.

"Michelle was perfect," he continued, referring to the woman who briefly captured his attention. "But after a while, I wasn't feeling she was worth the drive."

I exhaled slowly, preparing for what I knew would be an exasperating session. The Gardener, or rather "Michelle," had sounded sweet but firm, and like someone who could keep up with him. I found it hard to understand why he wouldn't be up for driving just a little bit farther to date someone he'd been uncharacteristically excited about.

"I can try to give you local matches only moving forward," I started, "but it's also my job to level with you. The idea that your dream woman just happens to live in your neighborhood is unlikely, at best."

"Not according to Aziz Ansari." He referenced a popular book the stand-up comedian wrote in 2015 along with the esteemed sociologist Eric Klinenberg.

"Did you even read *Modern Romance*?" I asked him skeptically. The book, one I love and recommend often, explores how dating has evolved over generations, and raises the topic of the paradox of choice. Having so many options, in large part due to the existence of dating apps, has made settling down feel more like "settling." Generations before us didn't have this problem, since most people just dated in their own hometowns and cities—something Kent was advocating for. I would have admired this bold, more traditional approach to finding love had it been coming from a motive besides laziness.

"Maybe I'm just an old geezer too set in his ways, and I'm better off alone." I smiled softly, recalling the email from Dave where he shared a similar sentiment with me shortly before our first date.

It was true Kent was older and used to his routine, but I was having a hard time believing that anyone who would fill out an extensive matchmaking intake, meet with me for an hour to share what he was looking for in a partner, and sign up for additional coaching sessions to have someone to unpack it all with, would be ready to just throw in the towel. Still, I wanted to give him the time and space to process his feelings surrounding his fatalistic conjecture.

Unsurprisingly, Kent didn't stay silent for long. "I'm just saying . . . ," he continued. "What if I already met the love of my life and I'm supposed to be punished forever for fucking it all up?"

Oh. This was new, I thought. *His feelings for Natasha are deeper than I realized.*

"Look," I started, moving to the edge of my seat a bit, "if you really felt that connected to Natasha before, maybe there's a way I can reach out to her and—"

"Whoa, whoa, whoa," Kent interrupted, seemingly appalled by the very notion. "You think I'm talking about *her*?"

"You're not?" *Who else could he be talking about?* I wondered.

"I'm looking for a woman with *passion*, remember? She told you what I said to her on our date, didn't she?"

I pursed my lips, amused. So he *had* known that Natasha had divulged his use of the L-word. The scamp. He explained that she was beautiful, her energy was great that night, and something just "took over" him on their date.

"Hasn't that ever happened to you before?" he asked, seeming certain it had.

"Kent," I leveled with him, "you say things out loud that most people just keep to themselves."

"We only live once, Jaydi. Why not shout 'love' from the rooftops if that's what you're feeling at the time?"

"Well," I answered calmly, "because if you're really feeling *love*, it won't just last a moment, will it?"

Some relationship experts recommend "the Twenty-Four-Hour Rule" following times of conflict. The practice involves providing yourself a window of time to process your emotions before reacting to a triggering situation with a partner. I believe this "rule" should also apply to intense positive feelings, such as the first time you think you feel love. Before you declare it to someone initially, I recommend waiting twenty-four hours. When you wake up the next morning, are you still feeling the same way? Or did that moment of passion pass? If it did, you've potentially spared your partner whiplash, and if it didn't, your words will still hold weight the next day.

Before giving Kent a lesson on this, I wanted to circle back to the aforementioned "love of [his] life," something he otherwise would have glossed over.

"I was talking hypothetically," he corrected me when I brought her up again.

"Sure." I stared into Kent's eyes, which were devoid of their usual sparkle of amusement. I'd been wanting to make progress with him for a while now, but always sensed there was something more he'd needed to move on from. I just didn't realize it was a *someone*. I felt a strong desire to know everything about the woman who had such a grip on what I thought was his previously inaccessible heart.

Like with Callie, I'd been so focused on helping him with his future that I hadn't spent enough time pushing to uncover his past. I started to wonder whether this was another blind spot of mine. I usually tried keeping conversations and advice focused on the present, believing that allowed for more immediate change (rather than indulging someone's preoccupation with their past, which was harder to alter). But the reality is that so much of who we are, and the decisions we make, are informed by ones we've made before.

Kent had spoken about his ex-wife so disparagingly that I doubted he still harbored feelings of love toward her. So were we dealing with something unrequited then? Or had Kent been referencing *The Notebook* all along for a reason? I could tell he wasn't ready to dive into that story today. But you better believe I was on a mission now to learn all about his Allie Hamilton.

ACT THREE

THE ANTAGONIST

Using a *tokkuri*, Dave poured sake into the small cylindrical cup before me at the sushi bar. He then handed me the vessel, expecting me to do the same for him. In Japanese culture, pouring your own sake is considered rude, and he felt compelled to honor the tradition at one of our favorite restaurants, Shibuya. I was happy we'd gotten seats so close to the holidays, given that Kim and Kanye were famously forced to wait a good thirty minutes for a table when they dined there. That was five years before, and the restaurant had only gotten more popular since.

"To babies," I toasted with him as we waited for our perfect pieces of bluefin toro nigiri to arrive. I wasn't going to miss alcohol during what I hoped would be an imminent pregnancy, but my newfound love of sushi was a whole other matter, and I was trying to pack it all in while I still could.

There was an older man beside us dining alone, and I wondered whether that would be Kent in ten years. I asked Dave how he would have felt if I had suddenly stopped seeing him because I decided he "wasn't worth the drive."

"You're talking to the guy who used to only date women on the West Side," he playfully reminded me.

"True." I'd forgotten how much he and Kent really were alike. "But in dating me, you realized you could explore a new part of town, you had somewhere to crash on the way home from work—"

"Yes. Because I *liked* you," he clarified.

"Liked?" I scoffed. "You were crazy about me."

Humor aside, I supposed he had a point. If Kent had been crazy about the Gardener, he wouldn't have minded driving to her—but from the sound of it, his feelings toward her had been overshadowed by the woman he was yet to get over. At least now there'd be more of a focus to our sessions.

I was also feeling optimistic about Callie, as she was still seeing Rachel, a set designer I'd introduced to her earlier that month. I was proud of her. Not only had Callie agreed to meet Rachel in the first place, despite bumping on her description (Rachel had two cats, and Callie had previously asserted she was only open to one), but she'd also given her another chance after Rachel had seemed a little too quiet on their first date—something old Callie would have classified as an "irrecoverable mistake."

"Maybe she prefers women," Dave teased when I gave him the update (he didn't know Callie by name, just some basic facts, and my frustration about her journey).

Before I could respond, I clocked an eerily familiar-looking blond at another table. "You've gotta be kidding me," I muttered.

Meera, who was sitting across from the guy, caught my gaze and froze, mid-laughter. I watched in fascination as Trevor shoved a piece of sushi into his mouth, licking his fingers afterward. *Gross.*

"Who's that?" Dave interrupted my stare.

"Oh, no one important," I said coolly. "Just two people I'm surprised to see here." I didn't feel like getting into the specifics yet, as I was too busy processing the scene. *Meera had emailed me they broke up. Did she continue seeing him anyway? Or did something change, and she forgot to update me? Was she ever going to update me? And why am I reacting like I just got cheated on? Get it together, girl!*

I averted my gaze and imagined Meera doing the same. I was reacting like a jealous girlfriend, which was absurd. I was angry, even though I didn't have a right to be. I'd laid out the perfect road map to happiness for Meera—something she'd been paying me good money to do—and there she was, choosing to ignore it. But why? Did she enjoy feeling hurt? Couldn't she see Trevor was just going to hurt her again, and likely soon? Within seconds, my anger turned to shame. *I didn't create a safe enough space for her*, I decided, *so she wouldn't feel judged for returning to him*. But that didn't excuse her not telling me, a person who'd been trying to help her, who only had her best interests at heart . . .

"Hello?" Dave politely reminded me of his existence as I continued to spiral.

"I'm sorry," I apologized. "You know how awkward I am when I run into clients." As a general rule, I try treating a client encounter the same way I would a stray dog: I don't engage with them unless they approach me first. I doubted Meera would do that tonight.

As my outrage subsided, I felt compassion take over for the sweet, deep-feeling, and forgiving Meera, who desperately wanted nothing more than to feel loved. I narrowed my eyes, watching as the object of her affection scrolled through his phone while she meekly tried to get his attention—and, for a moment, I contemplated chucking my kanpachi across the room at him.

I didn't cause a scene, though. Instead, I silently wished him food poisoning.

Meera had been tough to nail down in the New Year, but when she finally got around to booking another session with me, she was glowing. She and Trevor had spent a lot of time together over the break, and it seemed any chance I might have had to convince her to slow down with him had passed. She was riding the holiday high and focused solely on her potential with him now. We hadn't spoken yet about our encounter at the sushi restaurant: just because I had wanted to process our accidental run-in didn't mean she did.

My therapist taught me that three major questions lie at the heart of all major relationships: *Do you see me? Do I matter? When I reach for you, will you be there?* (Core considerations in EFT, or Emotionally Focused Therapy.) As I considered those questions now, I wondered how they applied to my coach-client relationship with Meera. Until then, I had been overly preoccupied with being "right" about their future—as if their having some sort of tumultuous breakup would prove my worth to her as her dating coach. Perhaps I'd been so intent on convincing her of the relationship's inevitable demise that I hadn't been supporting it, or her, the way I really needed to. So I decided to make a shift. I'd been seeing her, but was I really accepting her? When she reached for me, was I there unconditionally, or only when she was following my advice?

I started by apologizing for ever having made her feel like she couldn't come to me about Trevor—for making her worry I would judge her for doing something different from what we had discussed in our sessions. She stopped me before I went further, saying that while she appreciated my concerns, she'd never once felt judged by me. "I didn't tell you we were still seeing each other," she shared, "because . . . well, it felt stupid to do it. And it felt good to feel kind of stupid for a while, you know?" And then it dawned on me. Sometimes the safest space for anyone is the one that feels the most familiar. Healthy or not, that's what Trevor was to her.

"It's never stupid to follow your heart," I assured her gently. "That's a great quality." Meera saw the best in people, even those who might hurt her. She was the only one who'd have to live with the consequences of her decisions, and all the joys that came from them too.

"I'm just someone who wants what's best for you, and who has a ton of really good material for a speech at your wedding one day." I smiled. "That is, if you end up inviting me."

RECOVERING FROM HEARTBREAK

I'd been eagerly awaiting my final session of the day. Kent had kept me hanging after our last meeting, and ever since, I'd been dying to know more about this supposed One Who Got Away. If he took up half our session talking about his winery again, I was going to start drinking.

"Don't worry your pretty little head," he told me knowingly a minute or so in, "I'll tell you about Kate."

I got out my metaphorical popcorn and strapped in.

"She was perfect," he started, more seriously than I was accustomed to. "But really perfect. Not the bullshit I spew after a first date with a woman who wore a tight skirt, which as you know does quite a number on me. So it won't come as a surprise that I fucked it all up."

I waited patiently for more. Kent shared that they met when they were fifteen. Kate wore hand-me-downs from her sister and Coke-bottle glasses, but even with them on, he said, she was the most beautiful person he'd ever seen. Her dad gave him one of those "if you hurt my daughter" lectures later, but there was no point. "Only an idiot would hurt a girl like that," he confessed. "So I didn't. At least not right away.

"We were inseparable until eighteen, the summer before college. I was moving away, but told her I'd make it work. I would have driven hundreds of miles to see her back then." He closed his eyes, losing himself in the memory. "But that summer, my brother, Garrett, died."

For a moment, my heart caught in my throat. I'd never heard Kent mention a brother before, but as he collected himself, I could tell the loss had been immeasurably profound for him. "Kate was away when it happened, on vacation with her family or something. And my parents . . ." He trailed off, unable to put the impact into words. "No one could believe it. He was an honors student, class president who played lacrosse—because it wasn't enough to be smart *and* popular, right?" He allowed himself to chuckle. "He had to be athletic too. And it was all for nothing because he got into the wrong car at the wrong time."

He grimaced, and I was gutted for him. I had seen firsthand the lifelong scars this kind of loss can cause: my mom's sister died when she was pregnant with me, and my grandparents and aunts haven't been the same since.

"I had a lot to drink at the funeral." He powered through his story, and I understood. If he stopped, he'd probably shut down for good. "Kate was out of town, and that was who I really needed there. You know? But Garrett's friend Sandy, she was destroyed too. Like, absolutely wrecked, and drinking like the rest of us. And before I knew it, one thing led to another and . . ." His voice trailed off. "Kate tried to forgive me. But things were never the same again. I mean, how could they be? Even buying a ring for her after didn't change that."

I let out a small gasp. "You proposed to her?" *Kent? The man who could never commit?*

"She said yes, if you can believe it, but that didn't last long. Every fight, every argument . . . it just ended coming back around to what I did. And I deserved it too—her leaving me. She should be with a man who knows better than to ever fuck up something that good. I guess I'm just not capable of it."

"You were so young." I felt for the distraught boy inside Kent he still hadn't let go of. "You can't beat yourself up for one mistake forever."

"Oh, honey. I don't do that anymore. There is no undoing what I did." He got curious years later and looked Kate up on social media. She was married, apparently, with three kids, and even one grandchild. If he'd ever fantasized about getting back together with her one day, that ship had long sailed.

I agreed with him that you can't undo the past, but added that he still had time to build a beautiful future, with someone new. "Every love is different. I can't promise it will be the same as your first one, but I can promise you'll be glad that one ended. Because if it didn't, you wouldn't be able to feel the incredible love I know you'll feel again one day, the kind you can only feel after going through such an excruciating kind of heartache, one that will make you never take your next love for granted."

"Do they make you pass some sort of corniness test in order to become a dating coach?" he asked me cheekily. I had known, even as I was speaking, that Kent would have some sort of response like that. Even when recalling the most traumatic parts of his life, he still managed to maintain his sense of humor.

"I'm serious. You feel like you don't deserve Kate, but that doesn't mean you don't deserve love."

"Maybe. Or maybe I'm just meant to have flings with women half my age for the rest of my life. Are you saying I don't deserve to have fun?"

"*Is* it fun for you still?" I asked him blankly, genuinely curious. "How old is Kate now anyway?"

"She's my age. We went to high school together. Jesus, weren't you listening?"

"I was asking rhetorically," I told him slyly. "She's your age, which is exactly my point. Maybe it's time you start dating women your own age." The Gardener had been a step in the right direction, but even she was a full decade younger.

Kent grinned. "You're good, Jaydi. But not that good."

Dammit, I thought. Even on a day when he was feeling this vulnerable, I couldn't get him to reconsider. *Why is it people complain about being single, but categorically rule out fantastic someones who could potentially cure their loneliness forever?* The woman I'd been envisioning for him, Rita, would have to wait a little longer.

Later that day, I got word from Callie that she wanted to meet, and I happened to have a cancellation. She seemed in good spirits, and I wondered what the urgency was. She shared she recently got a promotion at work (amazing!), but that she'd also decided to end things with Rachel (boo). And in true Callie fashion, our exchange about it all raised more questions than answers.

"I realized I want to end up with a guy," she shared as casually as she would about her favorite flavor of ice cream. I couldn't help but feel amused. Dave's earlier speculation had been wrong!

I wasn't sure removing all women from Callie's dating pool was the answer, though, and worried that her breakup with the set designer was less about gender and more about her instinct to run away from someone once their connection grew deeper. Or maybe she was right to distance herself. We can't always point to *why* someone isn't right for us. Sometimes it's only a feeling. Before processing hers, Callie asked if I had any men in mind for her, and I worried she was being pulled in two different directions, both stemming from fear—fear of not getting to have children and fear of settling. The push and pull seemed to be constant, and always landed her in the same place: alone. I wondered who she could be once the shackles of fear were removed, and hoped I'd be lucky enough to witness that transformation. But currently, Callie was having trouble seeing past the looming expiration date of her membership, and worried she was no "better off" than when she first signed up with me nearly a year ago.

I worried her speculation discounted the growth I'd witnessed from her—growth that would help her better connect with the right partner. I also explained that she and I were operating under different timelines—mainly that she had one at all. That's not to say I lack a sense of urgency on behalf of my clients, but I'm unwilling to compromise the integrity of my search for a mutually desired outcome.

Callie had informed me from the outset about her plan to initiate IVF on her own if she wasn't willingly paired up with a potential life partner soon, and I respected she was disciplined enough to enforce the self-imposed deadline (something I normally advocate for). But I sensed that in a rush to make her dreams happen, Callie was delaying them more.

"What about a partial refund?" she asked, so innocently that it felt like a double gut punch. "I mean, for our remaining time together?"

I felt hurt and fury bubbling to the surface. The amount of behind-the-scenes work I'd done for Callie this past year was tremendous—not to mention our coaching work together that would have long-term benefits beyond just her membership. And never mind that our delayed start was entirely a result of her own self-sabotaging. *Besides*—I felt myself getting fired up—I had just introduced her to someone she hit it off with for thousands less than what most matchmakers charge!

"It's fine if not," Callie added uncomfortably, probably sensing my energy shift. "Just figured I could use all the funds possible if I'm going to end up going the IVF route." I allowed myself to feel compassion, imagining her anxiety. The thing she wanted most in the world wasn't coming to her as readily as she'd hoped, and that was scary.

I thought about other times I'd been blamed for someone feeling down about their prospects. I'd been inculpated for not setting someone up often enough, because they interpreted the lack of introductions as me undervaluing them. "*Am I not worthy enough for one of your bachelors?*" they've wondered, when oftentimes it's the complete opposite. I think so highly of them that I'd rather hold off for a stronger match than set them up for "the sake of it." Frequency is not an indicator of value when it comes to matchmaking. Quality is. And frequency can backfire, especially if there's a lack of chemistry present on the dates. "*This is how you see me? You think that's the best I can do?*" is a phrase I prefer to avoid.

Most notably, these frustrations are often expressed by our least confident clients. The others will usually brush off a "bad" date quickly, choosing to focus communication around how to improve the next one. Or they will check in if there's a lull between matches, and feel reassured hearing that we're holding out for someone we're excited about. Rather than internalize the feedback, I do my best to empathize with how a client is feeling—how I used to feel when I was single too, wondering if I was going to be one of those unfortunate people who winds up dying alone.

Callie was relatively confident, but her insecurity surrounding timeline was allowing fear to drive her decision-making. But I'm a fair person, and if I'd only set her up a few times by the end of her membership—even if part of that delay was of her own making—I'd be open to extending it for at least one more match. My investment in her also wouldn't end once her membership expired. "Just because I won't be your matchmaker at some point doesn't mean I won't still care. We both want the same outcome for you."

"Babies?" she asked me hopefully.

"Your happiness."

Endings seemed to be the theme of the day. To my surprise, Meera broke things off with Trevor. This time for good. He'd canceled their weekend getaway to Northern California to meet her family, citing that he was "too busy with work" again—and something in her finally clicked. Instead of crying during our session that followed, she looked focused, as if sheer determination alone could get her to suddenly move past the relationship she'd been pouring her heart into over the last year.

I was proud of her for ending it on her terms, since that was likely the only way the breakup was ever going to last. I'd seen far too many women and men in Meera's position actually marry the very person causing them so much pain, and was relieved she had decided to forge a different path for her future. I knew how much she'd been wanting Trevor to meet her family, and for the relationship with him to work out in general.

"Thanks for being there," she told me grimly. "I'm not sure I could have gotten through this without you."

"You followed your heart," I comforted her. "But maybe in the next relationship, we'll have your head do a little more of the leading."

"Or maybe you can lead?" she joked, and suggested I set her up with someone else as a distraction.

The benefit of waiting until you absolutely can't take it anymore to end a relationship is that it's possible to immediately feel ready to start another, a mindset I related to firsthand. I should have broken up with my ex years before I did, but the more friends and family tried convincing me he was all kinds of wrong for me, the more I doubled down and defended him. Behind closed doors, he and I would have all-out nasty brawls that would leave us both in tears, and we'd regularly confuse passion for intimacy. But he was extraordinarily persuasive. Every time I worked up the courage to break up with him, he'd somehow manage to convince me it was the wrong decision—and that everything would be wonderful again, if only we could start over. And so we did.

Finally, after three years of this insufferable dance, I successfully ended things over text. Worried he'd do what he always did, which was show up at my doorstep to try to win me back, I decided the only practical solution was to leave Los Angeles. I packed an overnight bag, told my two closest friends, and drove north without a plan. I felt suffocated, and thought the only way I could breathe easier again was if I left the city entirely. The air would feel fresher somewhere else, I reasoned—somewhere else not poisoned by the negative energy of my ex. It was the closest I'd ever come to having a breakdown. An hour or so into my late-night drive, I woke up my mom in Florida to share she'd been right about him all along. Rather than relish being "right," she did the most loving gesture possible in the moment: she looked up the safest place for me to pull over and get some rest.

I still remember the La Quinta in Bakersfield, wedged somewhere between the Sequoia National Forest and a Vallarta Supermarket, where I spent the night. In some ways, the move could have felt like a regression (during previous arguments, I'd spent nights at other hotels and friends' houses), but instead it felt like a rebirth. When I woke up with a clearer head, and my younger brother there for emotional support (he took the day off to drive up and meet me), I realized that geography wasn't the problem—nor was it my ex. The problem was me, and what I'd been willing to put up with. From that day forward, I channeled my inner Selena Gomez and decided I deserved better, and refused to settle for anything less.

I hoped Meera was in the same headspace. She asked me whether there was still time left to find her soulmate. I told her that of course there was, although I wasn't sure we had the same definition of the word. I believe there's a very limited number of men or women who can be right for any one person—and if you're with one of them long enough, your feelings might become indescribably deep, rendering happiness with another impossible. Essentially, you aren't born with a soulmate, but under the right circumstances, someone can become yours.

Meera thought that perhaps she should shift priorities to consider a person "good enough" instead. This philosophy is a hotly debated one, and more nuanced than the phrase itself suggests. I did think Meera was too focused on a superficial checklist, and could benefit from weighing a man's consequential qualities more heavily, but that didn't have to correspond with "settling." I told her as much.

"But what if the right guy for me doesn't exist?" she questioned gingerly.

"He does," I said, refusing to fuel her need for self-pity.

"How do you know? What if Trevor is the One Who Got Away?" I stared at Meera blankly, trying to figure out whether she was kidding. She broke a smile. "Okay, so he didn't 'get away.' I got rid of him. But if the right guy for me does exist, then where is he?"

"I can't tell you *where* he is, Meera. But I can probably tell you more about who he might be." I considered what I pictured for her. "I see you with someone around your age. Maybe mid-thirties or so. Someone close with their family, well traveled—more for work than wanderlust, probably. Practical, but who finds your romanticism endearing. Kind of the weight to your balloon, so to speak."

"A weight doesn't sound too fun," she interjected.

"It is if you'd float away otherwise! Or get pecked to death by a seagull."

"Are all your metaphors usually this morbid?" she wanted to know.

"About half of them." I smiled.

"Okay." She sat deep in concentration. "Does the weight look like Chris Hemsworth?"

"It could." I managed a laugh. But I told her I thought she was still too focused on looks. Attraction matters, but not if that's paired with toxicity. I'd been waiting patiently for Meera to show signs of progress, but until she got to the root of why she was so drawn to problematic matches, the only movement she was going to be doing was back into their arms. I suggested to her that she might not even realize the range of men she could be attracted to if they possessed the right energy or personality.

"I'm over thirty, Jaydi. Don't you think I'd know by now?" *Kent is almost sixty*, I wanted to shout. She also never had the experience of dating as the most confident version of herself, which I stressed to her would be a game changer.

"Then," I shared, "the most attractive thing about a person would be that they recognize your value."

"I hope I get to find out," she said with a twinge of sadness.

"You will. I know that sometimes, going on all these dates feels like spinning your wheels. But one of these days, you're going to experience the last first date you'll ever have."

THE CLIMAX (AKA THE LAST FIRST DATE)

Because I knew Kent wouldn't be receptive to meeting Rita, at least initially, I started planting seeds of her existence—like letting it "slip" that I thought the woman I was meeting right after him would actually be "perfect" for him. Naturally, he wanted to know more about her.

"Sorry, gotta go!" I teased. "She's already in the waiting room, but I'll see you again soon."

Slowly, I worked the understated Greek gem into our conversations. "She's the most amazing sound healer, whose main job is in finance. Such an interesting combo, don't you think?"

Kent scoffed. "I'm not sure I could take a sound healer seriously."

"Well, you would if she healed *you*," I asserted.

Then, I dropped the phrase that's pure kryptonite for people like Kent. "I thought about introducing her to you, but then I realized: she probably wouldn't be into it."

"What? Why the hell not?" He puffed out his chest, seemingly offended. "I'm the best."

"You're great," I agreed with him amusedly. "But she usually doesn't go for men your age."

"My age?" he wondered, somewhat affronted. "How old is *she*?"

"Your age," I answered, stifling a smile.

"But that's preposterous."

"Why? She says men your age aren't youthful enough. Of course, I pointed out there's exceptions. Like you."

"You're damn right me."

If I took every client's "checklist" as gospel, Brian wouldn't be in love today with Vega, who came from a culture he'd never been exposed to before; Destiny wouldn't be married to a man who makes less money than she does; and Kent wouldn't have finally gone on a date with Rita, whom at one point he would have considered an "offensive" six months younger than him. My job, at least some of the time, is to nudge clients out of their comfort zones and to challenge their occasionally limited worldviews in order to help them achieve happiness.

"That sound healer you mentioned before," Kent had followed up over email. "Think she'd grab drinks with me?"

She did, and he couldn't even wait until the morning after to gush about their date. I was ecstatic.

"Before we get into it, let me say you were right. She is my type: a great mix of quirky, deep, talkative, smart, and sexy. I was worried when you told me her age—but the truth is, I found myself thinking thoughts during the date that were the kind of thoughts people think about people they're attracted to. I enjoyed watching her order food with

very specific modifications and referring to how loudly the person next to us was talking. It reminded me of me. We made vague plans to see each other again before she goes to Greece."

Rita's feedback, however, was comically to the point: *"We had a good time. He seemed a bit off-put by our distance, though. What did he say about me?"*

As I lovingly imagined Kent's first date with Rita, I found myself revisiting the first one I had with Dave. As a teen, I'd always fantasized about being the lead in my own rom-com, but what I didn't predict was that my future husband would be the one to write it.

I still recall the black minidress and heels I wore that night, and the newfound confidence that came along with them, and my recent breakup. I carried—no, more like strutted—that energy down the steps of my West Hollywood apartment all the way to the passenger side of Dave's sleek Lexus sedan, where he stood waiting to open the door for me in his red-checkered button-down shirt. It's not every day that you get to literally pick up your matchmaker, and Dave was dressed for the assignment.

What's more, he'd made two reservations—one at Ysabel and another at Beauty and Essex—and asked which I'd prefer. I wound up selecting Ysabel (I'd gone to a networking event at B&E the year before, and loved the idea of trying somewhere new). We joke to this day about what would have happened had I chosen differently. Perhaps in a parallel universe, the valet at Beauty and Essex would have banged up his car, impacting his mood that night, or we would have been seated somewhere too noisy, and we wouldn't have ended up together.

"What can I get you, Tiger?" Our waiter addressed Dave with

enthusiasm. (Either "Tiger" was his pet name for every dapper-looking guy who dined at his establishment, or he detected our palpable chemistry.)

Despite Dave's questionable lack of relationship experience, his first-date etiquette was flawless. He ordered a variety of tapas that catered to my preferences and was a total gentleman. And he indulged me in a topic I normally encourage clients to stay away from on a first date: work. I was curious how he'd gotten his start in reality TV.

Funnily enough, it turned out that my cousin had been a contestant on the very first NYC-based show Dave ever worked on, called *Change of Heart*. The show featured various couples sent on dates with other people. By the end of it, they had to decide if they wanted to remain in their current relationships or if they'd had a "change of heart." When the mention of my cousin came up, Dave immediately looked concerned and asked what her name was—after which he excused himself to the bathroom. I was horrified. Alone at our table, I imagined every worst-case scenario, most of which ended with Dave making out with my adored older cousin (which would have been an absolute nonstarter for me). Why else would he have left so abruptly? Until that point, the date felt too good to be true. So, maybe it was.

Fortunately, Dave returned with an explanation not quite as bad as the one in my head. He remembered my cousin well, it turned out, because they're both around the same age, Jewish, and went to Syracuse. And, as fate would have it, she hooked up with another contestant in the back seat of the car Dave was supposed to be filming in.

"You shot a porn with my cousin?!" I nearly choked on my salad.

"No, no!" He turned bright red. "I never hit record. Plus, I was facing the road the entire time."

While the small-worldness of the situation was astounding, the image of my cousin getting hot and heavy in the back seat of a production car—while Dave and the driver, Jamie (a good friend of his), struggled not to listen—was not.

"Tell me something else," I said to him, in desperate need of a distraction. "What about another show of yours? Anything you created you're particularly proud of?"

He instantly lit up, telling me about a recent one he shot for VH1 called *Making Mr. Right*. I hadn't heard of it at the time, but incredibly, the series starred three assistant matchmakers. Their job was to guide fourteen men on their journeys to find love, but there was a twist: those three women weren't matchmakers at all, but rather single women on a mission to turn the contestants into perfect matches for themselves! While that's not exactly what happened with me and Dave—at least not consciously—perhaps the show encouraged Dave to give matchmaking a try in the first place. Without realizing it, he had laid the foundation of what would become his very own love story, and, consequently, mine. It was the rom-com I always wanted!

As he and I geared up later for my next embryo transfer, I wondered whether this was the beginning of our sequel.

THE LEADS LEARN THEIR LESSON, PART ONE

"Desire for a relationship is not the same as readiness." My colleague Carina's words echoed in my head, and I wondered whether the same reasoning could apply to any aspiration.

It was May 2021, and my body had rejected the remaining embryo at our original IVF clinic. (Even though we had healthy embryos waiting for us at the new clinic, I couldn't bear the thought of leaving another behind. Now, I'd have no choice.) *What is wrong with me?* I wondered as I got my blood drawn for the umpteenth time. I'd tried all the scientifically debunked superstitions that the doctor and her referrals had recommended: an injection of soya bean oil, egg yolk, and glycerin to prime my body; ingestion of gross herbal teas on the daily; legs in the air for twenty minutes following the transfer; and acupuncture the day of. Still, no amount of intervention had empowered my body to do exactly what I needed and wanted it to do most.

I felt defeated, and I thought about how applicable Carina's words were not only to my life but also to the lives of those I coached. When we started working together, Kent, Meera, and Callie craved the same universal, intangible, equal parts frustrating and fulfilling thing we call "love," and yet—at least some of the time—seemed to actively undermine their very chances at attaining it. But were they more ready to attract it now?

Kent appeared to be falling harder for Rita, evidenced by his unsolicited weekly updates to me over email. (*"I did it. I think I finally won over her cat."*) Since moving on from Trevor and having the clarity to truly unpack their dynamic, Meera seemed to decide that being treated well, consistently, was finally a turn-on for her—and while she was still skeptical of someone less passionate up front, she agreed it was no longer a dealbreaker. Even Callie reaffirmed her commitment to keeping an open mind on her search.

"You really think I could meet someone playing pickleball?" she asked me earnestly, a month shy of her yearlong membership expiring.

I responded encouragingly, and also recommended she try hiking groups, concerts, and dining meetups as well. If she connected with someone during any of those activities, she would know from the start that they had something in common (hardly a requirement but it certainly couldn't hurt). It also wouldn't be a wasted evening if she didn't meet anyone, because she'd already be partaking in an activity she enjoyed. I also suggested she consider hobbies or interests her future partner might like, even if they differed from her own.

"You might not be into sports, for example, but what if your future partner loved it? Would it really kill you to grab a drink at a sports bar one night with your friends instead of your usual wine bar?"

Similarly, men often overlook the power of showing up to a workout class typically populated by women (think yoga or exercise dance). While I recommend they wait until after class to strike up conversation with someone (most people prefer to focus on their workouts), this is another way someone can expand the circle of singles they're typically exposed to. Even if a woman you approach is "taken," your confident and adventurous spirit might inspire them to think of their single best friend they now want to introduce you to.

When it comes to dating in real life (IRL), which is rising in popularity again due to the decline of online dating and other factors, the possibilities are endless. Naturally there are bars, friends' birthday parties, singles mixers, and fun classes from pottery to stand-up comedy typically available. (I also encourage all my male clients to try speed dating, because those events are typically crawling with incredible women, while the quality of men there tends to be more suspect.)

But if all else fails, you can always get creative. Dave Cline, a twenty-eight-year-old data manager from West Philly, once spent a thousand dollars to rent a billboard in his neighborhood, asking women for dates. Hunter Lineberry in North Florida started following ChatGPT's suggestions of what he should do to find a wife, and posted the results on TikTok. Karolina Geits, a model and influencer, went viral for walking the streets of New York with her "looking for a husband" sign. And in a trend that gained popularity in 2022, read-only "date-me docs" became a long-form way to advertise who you are and what you're looking for in a partner. The dating CV is a nod to personal ads that used to get placed in newspapers—some look like dense résumés, filled with nothing but facts, while others sport sleek designs and look more like polished websites, even equipped with musical soundtracks.

Callie wasn't ready to try anything less traditional yet, but feeling inspired by our pep talk, she started averaging about six dates per week in a determined, last-minute frenzy; Meera, though, needed more nudging in this area. She was relatively more reserved to begin with, and less likely to walk up to attractive strangers and initiate conversation. She also felt differently about her finances than Callie, and believed that while free "outings" such as farmers markets or volunteer opportunities were worthwhile, memberships and paid activities at social clubs such as Soho House or Singles Only Social Club (SOSO) weren't a good use of her income. (If you do have the discretionary funds, though, I highly recommend it!) And let's face it: some events are worth splurging on. My good friend Danene attended my destination wedding despite not being in the best position to do so at the time. She even roomed with someone she didn't know well in order to make the trip more affordable. The result? She wound up meeting her husband that weekend, Dave's good friend Jay! That five hundred dollars ended up being well worth it.

Meera had an additional obstacle, though, at least in her eyes: her closest friends were all coupled up, and she felt uncomfortable attending any outings solo. My first step was convincing her to do it anyway. Even if she didn't wind up meeting anyone, simply stepping outside her apartment could yield other valuable benefits. Was she being more active than usual? Getting sunshine she might not ordinarily receive? Could she acquire a new skill? Or meet a new friend?

"Statistically, it's actually better going out alone," I pointed out the silver lining to her. When alone, women appear more approachable to men than when they're with their girlfriends. It takes someone *extremely* confident to walk up to your group of friends and strike up a conversation with you, whereas it's less intimidating if you're out by yourself. While having a partner who's confident in any situation would be great, your future husband might just be the kind of guy who would be more likely to walk up to you if you weren't surrounded by a sea of other women, analyzing his every move.

I stressed to Meera the importance of initiating conversation, and not to assume a guy wasn't right for her simply because he wasn't approaching her. This was apparent to me after all the men I'd coached, but not to Meera, who was self-conscious to begin with. She was more the type to attend an event and stand around uncomfortably, waiting for men to magically notice her. While that's fun to fantasize about, men don't approach women as much as they used to. In the age of swiping culture, with endless options at our fingertips, why risk possible face-to-face rejection? What's more, "in the wild," it can be hard to tell whether the person you have your eye on is even single.

"I'm not suggesting you go up to a guy and assert, 'Hey, you're cute. What's your phone number?'" I explained to Meera. "I'm saying if you're at the grocery store, maybe you go up to him and ask if he knows where the pasta sauce can be found."

"And then what?" she wanted to know.

If he was interested in getting to know her better, I told her, he'd do the rest. He'd bring her to the pasta aisle himself, or turn it into a conversation. If he had a girlfriend or wife back home, or simply wasn't interested in her, he'd say he didn't know, or point her in the right direction and leave it at that. Approaching someone takes confidence, and confidence is attractive—so at the very least, he'd respect the move.

"Just because you strike up conversation with him first doesn't mean he can't ask you out first," I highlighted. There are no hard rules when it comes to this stuff. Talking to a guy doesn't mean you're automatically flirting with him—he'll only read into your interaction if he wants to.

Meera was open to trying this, but for some of my clients, that's a step too far. For them, I recommend starting with approaching people they have no romantic interest in, to remove the stakes. For some, there can be a feeling of shame that comes along with being single, or a feeling of insecurity as they move through the world with this self-imposed label—as if their relationship status is as visible to others as their shirt. For them, kicking off a conversation with someone they're interested in can feel daunting. My client Teresa fell into this category. She was a widow who hadn't so much as flirted with a man other than her husband in forty years. By approaching women first, she was able to get in some conversational practice without the fear of consequence. Once she mastered that, she could feel more comfortable approaching men.

"So you understand your 'homework' then?" I playfully asked Meera, who nodded.

"Yup. Stop being afraid of the hot Starbucks barista?"

I laughed. If she could only channel the same confidence and humor she had with me, there'd be no looking back.

THE LEADS LEARN THEIR LESSON, PART TWO

As spring ended, I poured myself even more into client meetings and writing. The results were palpable, between more success stories and job opportunities, but once again this meant less quality time for Dave and me. Dave's primary love languages, or the ways in which he gives and receives love, are spending quality time together and acts of service—gestures that involve showing love through small, practical actions. They also happen to be the two that require me to give up more of my time, which was not something I felt I had the bandwidth to do at the moment.

The term "love language" was coined in 1992 by the Baptist minister Dr. Gary Chapman, in his book *The 5 Love Languages*, and has since become a central part of the conversation surrounding dating, relationships, and compatibility. In addition to spending quality time with a partner, and expressing acts of service, he also cites words of affirmation, gift giving, and physical touch as the other categories. (Two new ones emerged in 2022, following a dating trends report published by eHarmony: shared experiences and emotional security. However, I think those are just fancier ways of dressing up the original five. Shared experiences, which involve creating mutual memories with a loved one, feels like a subcategory of spending quality time with someone. And emotional security is something that should be a requirement in any healthy relationship—different from someone's primary way of giving or receiving love.) While all expressions of affection are wonderful, and usually welcome, not everyone feels love the same way. No matter how much we *think* we're expressing love to a partner, it will always land best if it's in the form of the other person's preferred love language.

Some dating experts believe you should find a partner whose primary love languages match your own in order to make communicating with them easier, but to do so would be to potentially write off other incredible partnerships. Instead, I advise you to discover what your significant other's love languages are, and adjust the ways in which you show affection to them based on that, and help them do the same for you. This could take work, but the reward in the end is worth it.

When Dave and I first started dating, our love language adjustment was real. No matter how much affection I'd show him physically or verbally, or how many thoughtful gifts I'd get him, none of it would be received as well as his coming home to clean dishes or our taking a hike together. Likewise, he didn't understand why I wouldn't instantly melt when he'd bring me flowers (my preferred love language is physical touch). Over time, we've adjusted, but I occasionally have to remind myself how far making him a cup of coffee before his daily workout will go.

Understanding the meaning of love languages is not only beneficial for a relationship: it can also help you grow as a person—after all, it's a widely held belief that our most toxic trait is the direct opposite of our primary love language. For example, if you value quality time, you might withdraw emotionally as a form of punishment, believing that isolating yourself is the most powerful way to make a point. Similarly, if your love language is words of affirmation, you might verbally manipulate your partner, or put them down, when your needs aren't getting met. If you prefer acts of service, you might resist asking your partner for help when you need it most. Rather than communicate a desire for assistance, you might handle everything on your own, but then later resent your partner for it. When gift giving turns toxic, you might overspend in an attempt to fill an emotional void. A new car or luxury vacation might make you feel better after a breakup, but you'll ultimately have to confront your feelings if you want to move on. Last is the avoidance of physical touch—something I suspect Meera was on the receiving end of before her relationship with Trevor. This category can include anything from someone withholding sex, to a mother refusing to hug her crying child. If your instinct is to retreat this way, it's important to be mindful about the effect it's having on the person you care about most. Like any toxic trait, this one can be worked on through therapy and a clear communication style.

Understanding your love languages can also teach you how to flirt more authentically. For instance, if you're comfortable with physical touch, you can signal interest to your date with a bold reach for their hand or gentle stroke of their hair. If you primarily use your words to affirm others, you might feel more comfortable dishing pointed compliments. If your love language is quality time, gift giving, or acts of service, know those traits can help make you an incredible partner, but they don't tend to lend themselves as easily to a flirting style (since they require a level of personal experience, knowledge, and intimacy that's impossible to have on a first date).

I often dedicate whole sessions to teaching singles how to flirt more effectively, but some skeptical bachelors or bachelorettes such as Meera wonder whether flirting is even necessary. (It is.) While Meera rarely gave a "bad" first date, men often parted ways with her unclear where they stood. That's because she was a magical thinker: someone who assumed her future husband would instantly recognize her heart, mind, and soul and risk everything to be with her before they even got to know each other. She expected prospects to work hard for the reward of getting to know her while offering little to no encouragement on her end. I eventually realized this was likely why she was drawn to such intense personalities—the types to bare their souls, whether solicited or not. But it was high time Meera stopped relying on chance encounters with Bares and started engaging with men who were better suited to her, which meant she'd have to start indicating interest of her own more.

When we discussed that, I shared with her my own history of struggling in that department. I too used to avoid eye contact with attractive strangers at all costs, terrified they'd read my mind and know I was interested in them (counterintuitive to my objective of getting them to approach me). I badly wished I could channel a more flirtatious energy like my friends Andrea and Katie or Emma Stone in the movies, but this simply didn't come naturally to me.

I once went out to dinner with a colleague, a traditionally handsome Broadway actor and activist I had a crush on, and only found out later that he'd been interested in me too. He treated our initial "date" as platonic, because I'd given no indicators of interest (something we cleared up with an actual date, a year or so later, which led to a goofy makeout session in a Korean sauna). Not until I started matchmaking, and heard feedback from thousands of other daters, did I realize how important it was to provide encouragement.

"At the very least," I suggested to Meera, "keep things light."

"But I'm a serious person," she expressed. "If I'm pretending to be some carefree cheerleader on our first date, isn't that deceitful? I don't want to be fake."

I explained to her that it was only fake if she never experienced joy. If she did, and of course she did, she simply needed to channel that same feeling on the date—revealing that side of herself earlier than she was accustomed to. So when did she experience unadulterated joy? We settled on the version of her who shows up to concerts. Concertgoing Meera was giddy, unencumbered, and delightful. Who wouldn't want a second date after meeting *her*? The ability to exude positivity and warmth on command is not only useful in romantic situations; it's also beneficial in friendships and professional settings. When your presence and personality are a value add, people want to spend more time with you.

"Okay, fine," Meera said, somewhat convinced. "But that's still not the same thing as flirting."

I was glad we were finally addressing this. We'd spent so much time in our sessions tediously unpacking bad behavior from men who were never going to make her happy in the first place that we had little time to add more skills to her dating arsenal. But now we could. During a previous session, we'd discovered that Meera's primary love languages were quality time and words of affirmation. The latter was something I could work with, and asked what came to mind in terms of a more verbal flirting style.

"I don't know. Banter, I guess. Giving someone compliments?"

I nodded. This was along the lines of what I usually hear. But compliments alone aren't enough to make the tone of a date feel romantic. The litmus test is: could their mom realistically say the same thing to them (e.g., "My son is so handsome. Aren't you impressed by his big promotion?")? Words of flattery are nice, but if your intention is to build more chemistry with someone, I recommend pointing out something their mother wouldn't. If an overt compliment about their hair feels too daunting (e.g., "women must want to run their fingers through it all the time"), I recommend a more subtle tactic: masking the compliment as a question.

"Imagine you're on a date with a guy," I instructed Meera, "and you say to him, 'So what do *you* do to work out?'" I adjusted the cadence of my voice to sound a bit more seductive. "Notice, I'm not asking the guy *if* he works out. I'm already assuming he does. If my husband were on a date with someone, and they looked him up and down and asked, 'So what do *you* do to work out?' he'd instantly light up and think, 'Wow! She noticed how toned my arms are getting from boxing!'"

When complimenting someone of either gender, it's important to comment on something you're noticing physically, in the here and now. It not only shows that you're present, but it also conveys the impression that you're liking what you see. It could be someone's smile, their eyes, or anything else about their appearance.

"More the face or body than what they're wearing," I expounded to Meera. "Guys are oblivious, and he might just think you like his fashion sense. That doesn't mean you're interested in *him*."

This was a deliberate point to make. Women may want to be viewed as more than just sex objects, but we often forget some men *don't*. By complimenting something about a guy's appearance, it subtly hints that physical intimacy might be a possibility down the road, which is likely to pique his interest. On the flip side, when complimenting women, I recommend emphasizing a choice we've made in addition to our more physical qualities. Highlighting our luscious hair or sultry eyes is gratifying, and I recommend doing it, but acknowledging the clothes we've *chosen* to wear on the date, or even asking a meaningful follow-up to something mentioned during our conversation, will help take your charm to the next level.

And always remember: compliment, don't criticize. Some people resort to teasing in an effort to cut tension, but forget to tread lightly, and some of it can land as mean-spirited. I'm firmly against negging, or giving backhanded compliments in an effort to seduce someone (for instance, telling a woman she'd look even more beautiful without her makeup on—a compliment at face value, but also a subtle message that she's not as pretty as she could be in that moment). This can undermine a person's confidence, making them more vulnerable and receptive to advances, but it'll turn off someone else more confident. Even if it does "work" on someone less self-assured, don't be that person contributing to someone else's lack of self-esteem.

Enthused by all the tips, Meera asked for more, so I launched into a spiel about phonetic convergence, which involves mimicking the other person's speech. If a guy's talking really loud and fast, you can too. It's probably not something they'll notice, but that subconscious similarity can sometimes tip the scales in your favor. Knowing when to flirt, in some ways, is as important as doing it at all. Men make up their minds pretty quickly in terms of whether they feel chemistry with someone, whereas women are more likely to have theirs changed. He's short? Bald? A little overweight? Maybe not what you originally envisioned, but if the guy's interesting or charming enough, he's got a *chance* of winning you over. But if a man isn't feeling initial chemistry with you, the uphill battle is often much steeper. So, if you don't indicate interest early, you risk their putting you in the "dastardly friend zone," as Kent called it.

This logic baffled Meera. "What if I don't know if I like them or not yet?" she wanted to know.

Up until now, I'd been encouraging her to keep her guard up, and my advice to flirt early seemingly contradicted that. I could see why, but I wasn't against her giving signals she was interested in someone on a date—I was against her indicating she wanted a *relationship*. I wasn't advocating that she flirt for the sake of it. If she knew from the jump she had zero interest in someone, I agreed that would be disingenuous. But withholding enthusiasm entirely could cause someone—someone she might decide she likes later—to write her off. A little flirtation early on would buy her enough time to formulate an opinion on them, and the ball would be in her court about whether they would have a second date—something she reserved the right not to accept. Flirting isn't misleading when you're *unsure* about someone: it only is if you know you don't like them but flirt anyway.

I planned to expose Meera to a more physical flirting style too, but right now, I was worried about overwhelming her. We'd been covering a lot this session, and I wondered how much of our conversation would stick. Intellectualizing advice is one thing, but putting it into practice is quite another, especially when it might feel a little uncharacteristic and scary. I knew if we eased into it later, though, I'd be able to clear up some misconceptions when it came to flirting nonverbally, like believing that you have to literally touch another person for the style to be considered physical (which isn't necessarily true). You can touch yourself—not like that, get your head out of the gutter!—such as by twirling your hair, moving it to reveal the nape of your neck, or bringing food to your lips. Like leaving your hands on the table, a subtle hint that you'd be receptive to touch, these are all subconsciously inviting signs, helping to build a further sense of intimacy. You often see men do this by puffing out their chests. If you're on a dinner date and feel particularly daring, ask to sit beside your date, rather than across from them. This could be from the outset or when you return from the bathroom (perhaps even framing it as a way to hear them better).

Deploying the "triple nod" is another great physical indicator of interest. In fact, it's been proven that people are likely to speak three to four times longer if their conversation partner offers three slow nods after they've finished talking. It sends the message that you're interested in what they're saying, and more is welcome. Nodding also helps to build what scientists call a "yes set," meaning the more often someone agrees with you, the more likely they are to answer "yes" to your subsequent questions, such as "Do you want to see me again?"

Mirroring a partner, also known as the Gauchais Reaction, is another subtle way to engage. This limbic synchrony of copying body language helps to generate feelings of similarity with another person—something that can help foster attraction. Mirroring is something we do instinctively as early as infancy, as our heartbeats naturally sync up with our moms' rhythm. Mirror neurons in our brains also play a key role in empathy, giving us the ability to better understand another's experience, and enabling us to connect with them on an emotional level.

But these actions don't have to be subconscious. When mirroring men, it's better to mimic their body and not their face, since men are inherently less expressive and tend to rely less on facial cues. For all genders, I recommend "fronting"—squaring your body so you're directly facing the object of your affection. This builds a much stronger connection than standing shoulder to shoulder with someone. By facing them, you're making them the actual center of your attention.

What you *don't* do can be equally powerful in terms of conveying interest. Avoid crossing your arms, which might unintentionally indicate you prefer keeping your distance. If objects such as phones or vases are between you and a potential love interest, move them, as they can be mental barriers in addition to physical ones. Also, don't shy away from eye contact. According to Dr. Kerstin Uvnäs Moberg, in her book *The Oxytocin Factor*, locking eyes with someone else releases oxytocin, the "cuddle chemical" or hormone most closely associated with trust, sexual arousal, and relationship building. An affectionate pat on the back or playful nudge on the arm can do this too, provided it's welcomed. If someone withdraws, even in the slightest, when a physical overture is made, I wouldn't try again. Similarly, too much eye contact can make someone else feel uncomfortable.

This is all really complicated and confusing, so remember: it is for your date too. This is why, for women especially, being the one to break the touch barrier is useful—a gesture as simple as brushing a crumb off your date's collar will indicate you're okay with them expressing affection back. To those on the opposite end of the spectrum, those naturally affectionate with everyone, including waiters, be mindful that you preserve those gestures for your date alone. Otherwise the person you're crushing on might brush off an overture as being part of your personality rather than indicative of your interest.

The majority of my clients are like Meera, though, worried if they attempt anything less natural to them that they'll come off as awkward. This is where practice comes in. The same way we have verbal vocabularies, our bodies have physical ones. A new word isn't usually ingrained in our vocabularies until we start to use it regularly, and the same holds true for new behaviors and movements. To help my clients do this, I suggest they schedule virtual dates with singles on dating apps or otherwise—something men and women have been more receptive to ever since the pandemic (the date costs no money, and daters can meet someone new while wearing comfortable clothes—not to mention taking advantage of Zoom's "touch up my appearance" feature).

When chatting, I recommend placing an object out of the camera's view, beside your computer screen—for the purpose of the exercise, let's say your cell phone—and pretend it's your date's arm. Then, act as if you're in a movie. When it's time for the ingenue to laugh playfully, to brush the man's arm and say, "That's so funny," that's when you'd make contact with your phone. Your date can't see it, but the more you make contact with the phone during appropriate moments, the more your body will start to associate playful feelings with the need to touch something, or someone. Before you know it, you might feel comfortable trying this on friends or family or even on an in-person date. These virtual dates are great practice for learning how to flirt better nonverbally, something ironic given the physical barrier of the computer screen, but there's a built-in bonus too: you might really hit it off with the person you meet through it!

Before Dave came home from work that day, I'd just wrapped another lesson with a client on using love languages to her advantage. With it top of mind, I quickly cleaned off the kitchen countertop. And when Dave walked in, I asked whether he wanted to eat dinner together before my next meeting.

THE PREDICTABLE ENDING

Lying on the surgical table, I told myself this time would be different. And it needed to be. I wasn't sure how much more poking and prodding I could take. As the staff prepped me for what I hoped would be my last embryo transfer, my mind drifted to the photos Kent had recently emailed of Rita with his kids.

He'd introduced them all recently, and it seemed the meeting couldn't have gone any better. He'd been dating her for three months, and already he told me he was "in love." The pace felt quick, but not as quick as his misstep with Natasha. And in my experience, men move faster at his age—for better or worse. Perhaps it's the "what do I have to lose?" attitude that comes with getting older. That's not to say that's an indicator of possible relationship success. A couple I'd introduced in their sixties and seventies had gotten engaged in this same time frame. "Every day it gets better," the bachelor emailed me about his match shortly before proposing to her—only for the engagement to dissolve within the year.

Nicholas Wolfinger, a sociologist at the University of Utah, studied data from the National Survey of Family Growth, and found that the best age to get married with the least likelihood of divorce is between twenty-eight and thirty-two. The idea is that people in this demographic are "not too old and not too young," something those in his field refer to as the "Goldilocks theory." Below twenty-eight, people might not be old enough to distinguish between true love and puppy love, nor have they had as much time to get their careers and finances in order before focusing on family. Their ability to make long-term decisions might also be compromised given that the frontal lobe is the last part of the brain to mature—something that can happen as late as thirty. Yet, as people grow older, they become more firmly set in their ways, and are less likely to adjust to life with another person, which is problematic for marriage.

Still, I've known and introduced many exceptions, and was optimistic about Kent and Rita's chances. I'd carefully vetted any potential deal-breaking obstacles for them ahead of time, and his continued interest in her demonstrated his emotional growth. The former Kent, more nitpicky, had been chasing the idea of someone else—someone whom he'd lost decades ago. But with Rita, he was wanting to get to know the real her, imperfections and all, without comparing her to an idealized version of a ghost. He was even spending time in her stomping grounds in Calabasas!

Meera had also begun seeing someone promising: a Midwestern professor with a receding hairline, who was consistently displaying encouraging behavior. They'd met at the movies, waiting in line at the concession stand before a showing of *The Forever Purge*. After Meera struck up a conversation with him by commenting on the colorful pattern on his shorts, he made the bold move of suggesting they sit together in the theater. What started off as a horror film quickly turned into a romantic one.

I was elated for Kent and Meera, but like a mother who can only ever be as happy as her least happy child, I was feeling some misplaced guilt about Callie's unchanged relationship status.

"Do you think," she asked me minutes into our last scheduled Zoom together, "it's impossible to have it all?"

We had reached the end of her membership, and I wasn't surprised by the question. I hesitated to answer, despite knowing exactly what she meant. I thought about my marriage, my dating business, and my writing career—and wondered whether I was greedy for wanting to have a kid too.

"Is that what you think?" I asked her in an attempt to stall.

She thought about it. She was thriving professionally and owned a "really sweet condo"—but declared that neither would've been likely if she had gotten married and had a kid years ago. "Yup. It's impossible to have it all," she declared, "unless you're Gwyneth Paltrow or something."

"Well, Gwyneth Paltrow got divorced once," I pointed out. "Or rather, consciously uncoupled. Take it from someone who's worked with plenty of A-list celebrities: most people feel they're missing *something*, at some point."

Callie was echoing sentiments I've heard expressed by countless other colleagues and clients, from surgeons to public figures, who've each experienced their fair share of broken marriages and hearts—including those who appear happiest in the media. The presumption they should "have it all" is omnipresent during our conversations, and every day they haven't achieved that, they feel like a failure. I considered pushing back on Callie's premise, insisting that it *is* possible for a person to "have it all," but was that what I really believed? To excel professionally requires intense dedication, focus, and time—the same traits needed to sustain a happy marriage and family. Both require 100 percent effort, and the moment your attention is divided, something gets compromised. Perhaps Rihanna said it best when she revealed, "You almost feel like something is always suffering for you to show up somewhere."

But maybe that was okay. After all, we can't all be Michelle Yeoh and be everything, everywhere, all at once. Perhaps the key was to have it all . . . a little bit at a time. I thought about a friend of mine who went to clown school. I'd seen him juggle, and had been mesmerized as he maintained five balls in the air at once. But I also knew he hadn't thrown up all five simultaneously to start (if he had, the act wouldn't have lasted very long). Instead, he'd waited until he could successfully juggle three—then four, and eventually five. Even after knowing he could maintain all five in the air, he'd always start his act slow, with that same build.

Similarly, shortly after meeting Dave, my writing career seemed to slacken. Looking back, I don't think the timing was a coincidence. Dating Dave, my eventual life partner, was time-consuming. Windows of time I used to devote to work were instead spent primping for dates, and eventually mailing our save-the-dates. That's not to say I didn't have a healthy work-life balance, but I admit I pursued our love story more aggressively than the one I was pitching to networks at the time. But after our relationship had a secure enough foundation, I was able to focus more on work again.

I challenged Callie to recall when she was first starting her career—when she was writing coverage on scripts, making coffee, hustling, and working late, even after less qualified people were getting promoted before her. She worked her butt off, at the expense—she might argue—of having a personal life. I paused for dramatic effect, and asked whether she'd put nearly the same time into finding her partner.

She admitted she hadn't. "Like you said, how could I?"

I encouraged Callie to think of her life in three categories: work, self-care, and family. "You can *eventually* have it all," I suggested to her. "But first, you have to lay the proper foundation in one area before you can turn your attention to another. You've done that now with work. It's time to put a little more focus on yourself, and finding your partner."

I wasn't suggesting Callie neglect work entirely. But like my friend in clown school, she needed to throw the work ball in the air and tend to the other categories before that ball hit the floor.

"I guess my mom never threw that ball up in the first place," she said.

I was shocked at the extemporary accusation, and somewhat hopeful. For a while, I'd been wanting to hear more about Callie's childhood, but I knew it needed to come up organically. Still, I didn't think it would happen during our final session together. "She was in med school," Callie continued, "and basically gave up her dream of becoming a doctor when she got pregnant with me. She dropped out and never went back."

"Well, maybe that's because her dream was to have you." Even as I said it, I felt the inadequacy of the cliché. I reminded her that some women return to school even after having a kid. "It's really hard, but people do it, if that's what they really want. I don't know your mom, though, and maybe she was happy focusing all her time on family."

"She wasn't," Callie responded brusquely. "She gave everything to her marriage, and to her kids. And after she caught my dad cheating, she could barely figure out how to support herself. She could have been a doctor, if she took a different route. Instead, she wound up working in his office just to pay the bills. It was humiliating, but she wasn't qualified for anything else."

I sympathized with her, and better understood her decision to focus so much on her career—a valid decision even without her family history. Knowing why Callie pursued the path she took, and perhaps why she was so critical of people when she first met them, was instrumental in helping her on her journey. By trying to identify what was "wrong" with someone before diving into a relationship with them, or even a friendship, Callie had subconsciously been trying to avoid feeling trapped in the wrong dynamic, the way she perceived her mother was. But certain red flags can't be detected ahead of time. And sometimes, what is "wrong" with a person is actually what helps make them uniquely suited to another.

"You've been trying to avoid feeling hurt for so long that you've also been inadvertently avoiding feeling love. You deserve to feel love, Callie."

A single tear rolled down her cheek. By the time she realized it was there and wiped it away, only a few seconds had gone by—but to her, that demonstration of vulnerability was longer than she was comfortable with.

"I know that," she sputtered. "I mean, duh. I'm awesome, right?"

I wanted to reach through the screen and hug her. She really was. I wondered whether I would ever see her again, or whether—because I'd failed to meet her arbitrary timeline—I'd have to accept that my role in her journey to find love was over. She wasn't the type not to "make good" on her ultimatum. Still, I couldn't bear the thought of us parting ways after this breakthrough conversation, and asked if she'd be open to one more session with me, on the house, to at least talk through the next steps she'd be taking on her own.

"Really?" She seemed touched.

"Really." I saw a change in Callie that day. I had no way of knowing for sure, but something in me felt certain that the match she'd been waiting for was just around the corner—and I really wanted to be there when it happened.

THE RESOLUTION

When Callie didn't show up for her complimentary session, I was concerned. Our last one together had been fairly emotional—a state of being Callie tends to run from—but I hoped she recognized, and appreciated, the potential her growth unleashed. The ability to express her more vulnerable side was not only a healthy development for everyday life; it was also a requirement for any long-lasting relationship. By opening up about her parents' failed marriage, the invisible obstacle that had been preventing her from having a meaningful connection with another, I hoped that she'd finally start to heal and move past it.

I wondered whether she was avoiding me intentionally, or whether some emergency had prevented her from sending a courtesy email cancellation. I deal with no-shows occasionally, with reasons ranging from an unexpected death in the family to a poorly set alarm clock, and hoped it was the latter today. I tried to put her absence out of my mind, assuming I'd hear what happened soon enough. Besides, work was insanely busy, and I was grateful for the unexpected time to catch up.

Before shifting gears, I perused the Google Doc I share with Lauren to see if I had any outstanding dates to schedule. I smiled at the long list at the top of the couples we matched who were actively dating, followed by my list of coaching clients. My eye stopped on Meera's name, and I smiled at the matchmaking "hold" placed beside it. She had just reached the one-month mark with the Midwestern professor from the movies, and asked for me to withhold other introductions for now.

"You'd be proud of us, Jaydi. We're moving at a normal pace," she'd informed me. So far, the two had seen each other a handful of times, and no premature declarations of love had been made. "I do think he could be the One, though," she added. (At least she was telling me and not him. *Progress!*) While I wanted her to keep her options open, she seemed to be navigating this situation with a clear head.

Until now, based on what Meera had disclosed, the Professor hadn't demonstrated any red flags to worry about, and his intentions with her seemed pure. He expressed healthy curiosity about her life and desires, and most important, he listened, such as when he brought her daffodils because she shared her favorite color was yellow. If this momentum continued, I guessed they'd be calling each other "boyfriend" and "girlfriend" by month three.

I asked whether they were both on the same page with religion and politics, and they were. "He's not Hindu, but he's down to raise our kids that way—at least in terms of exposing them to all my family's traditions and culture. I don't mean *our* kids, literally." Her face fell, as if she caught herself. "Just kids in general."

"Don't worry." I smiled amusedly. "I'm not judging. It sounds like you two have a very healthy communication style." I appreciated how different this dynamic seemed from the relationship she was in a year ago.

Next, I probed into her physical, emotional, and intellectual connections with the Professor, and it sounded like each category was stronger than the last. (They hadn't yet been intimate with each other, but they'd fooled around a bit and he seemed okay waiting for more.) They hadn't experienced conflict yet, either—a positive thing given their short timeline—but I'm a fan of seeing how someone handles a disagreement, however minor, before becoming exclusive with them. Knowing whether that person has a tendency to shut down or work through conflict is helpful.

"But don't initiate a fight for the sake of it," I cautioned Meera jokingly. "Enough happens in life that you'll experience something to work through soon enough."

Our therapist taught Dave and me that most relationships have a conflict cycle: a repetitive pattern of blame and negative reactivity. What one person says to defend themselves may inadvertently hurt the other, and that person's reaction, in turn, has a similar effect. The basis for the argument itself might be slight—or the result of a simple miscommunication—but once this feedback loop starts, it can be difficult to end it. According to Dr. Sue Johnson, founder of EFT, conflict cycles are composed of four identifiable parts. The first is an attachment wound: how we've been hurt in our lives informs how we perceive the actions of others. (If you were neglected by your mother as a child, you might react even more negatively if your partner needs to leave the room to regroup, as this can trigger feelings of abandonment.) The second part is primary emotion: the feelings that arise because of our attachment wound. ("How dare you, person who claims to care about me, abandon me while I'm feeling upset and vulnerable. This makes me feel angry and extremely sad.") Without realizing it, this seemingly minor argument is reinforcing your attachment wound. The next part is defense mode. To protect ourselves, we react by fighting, fleeing, or freezing—all behaviors that might elicit a strong response from our partner. Lastly, we do something protective—the manifestation of our defense mode. If your instinct is to fight, you might yell at your partner, or even share some low blows, all of which could trigger something regarding their own attachment wound. These are just some examples of a conflict cycle. Every couple has their own unique one, and identifying yours is a requirement for being able to break it.

In the past, Meera had shied away from conflict entirely, and I'd encouraged her to choose a different path moving forward. All not voicing her concerns to Trevor did was delay the very outcome she'd been trying to avoid. The right partner, I'd explained to her, will *want* to know what's bothering her, so they have an opportunity to fix it.

But this meant she couldn't just presume intent. Similar to how she'd expected men to magically know she was interested in them before, she expected her partner to know when she was upset with him. Being in a relationship with someone who understood this, and was interested in learning her nonverbal cues surrounding conflict, was vital as Meera continued to work on improving her ability to speak up. I also anticipated some degree of overcorrection on that journey, but it felt too premature to caution her. I'd address that in due time, if necessary.

I prepped Meera on other precursors to exclusivity, such as being on a similar page with marriage and kids. She and the Professor seemed to be, which was great. (One of my friends, a man who wants children, recently married someone uncertain about having them. His spouse's hesitation might eventually resolve the way he hopes, or it could lead to divorce. Why roll the dice on something so fundamentally important?)

When it came to number of partners, Meera assumed he preferred monogamy. I told her she may want to clarify—after all, we were living in LA, a place where ethical nonmonogamy was really picking up steam. Lastly, I suggested she look for signs of future planning. If the Professor tried making plans together for weeks, or even months from now, it would indicate long-term thinking. Meera didn't seem worried, though. They already had plans to see each other twice the following week, and there was a calmness to her, as if he had somehow managed to quell her typical anxiety surrounding pace. In some ways, that change in her was a clearer sign than any others on the checklist I provided that her relationship had the legs to move forward.

Regardless of how it would pan out, I was thrilled she was departing from similar patterns and types of men. She seemed excited to be treated consistently well now, and was accepting the Professor's doting without resistance, another sign to me that she was feeling more confident and worthy of a more mature kind of love. I also suspected she'd be okay if this relationship didn't work out, because ultimately, she was beginning to truly love herself—the only guidebook she really needed.

This felt like a new chapter in Meera's life, and I couldn't wait to see how it ended.

It turns out I'd be entering a new chapter too. I stared at the plus sign on the pregnancy test in our kitchen, but my brain wasn't really processing its meaning. I took the test to confirm the news the nurse had just shared with me and Dave over the phone.

"Congratulations, Mama," I remember her saying.

It all seemed unreal. My body felt the same as the times the embryo transfers failed before. Shouldn't I *feel* a baby inside me now? And what was our plan? We worked so hard to make the pregnancy happen, we had barely focused on what to do afterward. But maybe that was okay.

I don't think Dave had thought much past proposing to me before doing it, nor had I before I accepted. While he'd been toying with the idea of marriage for a while, a short conversation with his uncle in the ocean was what inspired him after we'd only been together for eight months.

"So, what do you think?" he had asked Dave. "You think she's the One?"

"I do," Dave responded, watching me fondly as I read a book to his little cousin Blair on the beach.

"So what are you waiting for?" his uncle had asked curiously.

There was so much left to learn about each other. *Do we have similar thoughts on finances? Is Dave okay with my career as a freelancer? What are our expectations surrounding domestic roles? Do our families get along? We know we want kids, but do we share the same idea on timeline? How do we handle stress, and do we involve our partner in our processing of it?* The questions were endless, but one thing was certain: we enjoyed answering them as a unit. We were a team, and a damn good one at that.

As Dave initiated a FaceTime with our families to share the exciting update, any fears I had surrounding the pregnancy instantly melted away. Just like before, we may not have all our questions answered about the road ahead, but I knew that whatever it entailed, we would be able to get through it together.

THE DENOUEMENT

I'd been keeping my pregnancy news from my clients, convincing myself that while a quick flash of my engagement ring might feel aspirational for some, a baby bump might be a step too far—at least for women like Callie who desperately wanted children. (Fertility clinics are known to ban kids from their waiting rooms for this very reason.) I couldn't hide my good fortune at the next industry meetup I attended, though, especially because an in-the-know colleague had already spilled the beans to everyone before I even got there. Normally I might have been upset, but thanks to the welcomed subsiding of my raging hormones in the second trimester, I only felt positive energy that day. In fact, I barely cared when Dana started peddling more hot air about her still-super-top-secret technology, and even chimed in when Melody started bragging about a recent magazine profile.

"She's amazing, isn't she?" I heard myself gush about her. (And I didn't gag after.)

I was particularly delighted to see Daliya, a redheaded comedian-turned-therapist who was a couple of months away from pushing out a baby herself, and planned to mine her for advice. International Jewish matchmaker and a US Dating Awards' "Best New Dating Personality" winner, Jessica from Fass Pass to Love, was also present, along with Jenny from Jenny Apple Matchmaking. Those two were the first to immediately embrace me in the community and offer valuable words of advice. Jess, who always left a memorable impression with her signature glasses and Mayim Bialik–style delivery, sat across from me, and I listened amusedly as another matchmaker complained to her about an industry-wide "problem."

"Can you believe it? I matched her successfully after two months, and now she wants a partial refund because she still had time left on her membership! I'm like, girl, are you kidding me?"

"That's ridiculous," Jess agreed. "Next thing you know, she won't even tip you when they make it to the chuppah!" She referred to the canopy Jewish couples customarily stand under when they get married.

Some matchmakers go so far as to make tipping a requirement in their contracts, provided they make a successful match. Tips are another way for a matchmaker to optimize revenue, but one that leaves me feeling conflicted. In a twisted way, forcing a tip feels like "punishing" someone for finding love, and the last thing I wanted to do was disincentivize anyone. (I imagined a male client being on the fence about a possible second date with someone, but rather than considering the near future only, he opts to reject her, because he can't imagine a world where she'd be worth the thousand-dollar tip later.) That said, I'm a bit envious of those who insist on tangible proof of gratitude for our Herculean efforts, and I'm constantly reevaluating.

"Hopefully she'll at least let you post about it," I willed. "If they end up getting married." I considered that a win, since most couples I'd matched over the years didn't even want their names mentioned on my website. Some people feel a stigma about being introduced by a professional dating service, the way some early adopters of online dating used to. "We met through a friend," they'd tell others. Or "at a bar." But I could sense all that starting to change.

We had a couple more spirited discussions, including one about the "Three-Day Rule." (The theory stipulates that waiting three days after a first date is optimal before contacting a romantic partner. Reaching out the next day supposedly makes you appear too eager, and experts claim texting or calling on the second day feels calculated, making the third day the "sweet spot" to reach out.) I smiled, recalling a similar conversation I had with Kent.

"Why wait three days when you can make 'em wait five?" His eyes twinkled, as they often did when he was soliciting a reaction. "Make 'em sweat a little, don't you think?"

I doubted he intentionally made Rita sweat in the anxiety-inducing kind of way since they started dating. Meeting her had helped him become the best version of himself, and last I heard, he was in the process of moving into her Calabasas home with her and her cat.

While I think the "Three-Day Rule" could work with someone on the fence about you, if you have an obvious connection with someone, and they're ready for a relationship, they'll be glad to hear from you sooner rather than later. I'd also encourage you not to write off someone who didn't contact you "soon enough." It's possible they were preoccupied with something else important, or were given bad advice!

Before we could settle the debate, Bianca—who, I have to say, was wearing an especially chic pantsuit today—broke in to boast about the newest client she'd just signed: a former news reporter who'd been married to a professional athlete.

"Wait, you're not talking about Kimberly, are you?!" I exclaimed mirthfully.

"Oh my gosh, yes!" Bianca squealed with a mixture of excitement and surprise, like a pirate who stumbled upon a treasure box only to discover some coins had already been taken. "Don't tell me she tried you too."

"For a short time, but I ended up referring her out."

"Same, same!" Jessica interjected.

"Oh no." Bianca frowned, realizing her "amazing" new client was already known in our community. "I loved her during her intake. But now I feel like I should be worried."

"No," I assured her. "Kim is great. She's just exceptionally picky."

"I know." Bianca groaned, recalling the specifics. "She said no short dudes, liberal ones, or men who live west of the 405. Even though her mom does."

"I'm just glad she's your client now and not mine," I chuckled, and meant it. From what I could tell, Bianca seemed genuinely invested in helping Kimberly find a partner.

"What about that film publicist client of yours?" she asked me earnestly. "Did you ever end up finding her someone?" I was shocked. I'd only briefly passed Meera's photo around at the last gathering, and wrongfully assumed that most of my colleagues hadn't been paying attention.

"*I* didn't," I shared truthfully. "But she did meet someone on her own, and I'm optimistic."

"Was she a coaching client of yours too?" I nodded. "Good for you, Jaydi. That has to feel so rewarding."

I couldn't believe I was vibing with the same woman from one of the matchmaking corporations I took such issue with only a year before. Maybe Maria Avgitidis, Michelle Jacoby, and Laurie Berzack, cofounders of the Matchmakers Alliance—a not-for-profit organization and powerhouse community for dating professionals to network and collaborate—were onto something. We all have a lot to learn from each other. Some of us cling to a traditional approach. Others perform shamanic water spirit healing or program their own computer algorithms. But despite our differences, we all share a rare understanding of the incredible times when two clients we've introduced get engaged or name a baby after us—and the soul-crushing days when it feels like we're getting berated by the very people we're trying to help most. To celebrate the joys and—let's face it—to troubleshoot, we'll always have each other.

A couple of months later, I was thrilled when Meera invited Dave and me on a double date. Her suggestion, Shibuya—where we had our prior run-in—was intentionally comedic. I'd never been "asked out" by a client before, and wasn't quite sure how to respond. In the end, the temptation was too much for me to ignore, and I excitedly took her up on the offer.

The professor Meera was seeing was named Max, I learned, and between Dave and me, we probably made one "Miramax" joke too many—fitting, if you ask me, given that the happy couple met at the movies. Apparently, unlike some clients who "hide" their matchmaker, Meera proudly shared with Max tidbits about her journey with me, and he was the one who'd suggested including Dave and me in their six-month-anniversary dinner.

"Does it feel weird?" Max asked. "Running into Meera here on purpose?"

"Actually, it couldn't feel more right—even if I can only eat veggie rolls." I rubbed my now very pregnant belly for added effect.

As Max toasted to the exciting updates in all our lives, I felt incredibly proud. When I first met Meera, she was walking around in a constant state of mourning for a life she felt she deserved to lead, unsure whether she would ever have it. She was metaphorically unconscious, waiting for her Prince Charming to rescue her. Now, thanks to rescuing herself, she was getting treated like a princess. While I liked to think I played a small part in her transformation, she ultimately had to be the one to love the person she was, and will continue to be. She also had to decide how she wanted to be treated. And like I had decided after my drive home from Bakersfield, she had to be willing not to put up with anything less.

As the men got to know each other, Meera's phone rang, and I noticed the name "Trevor" pop up on her screen. If she seemed surprised, she didn't show it. Instead, she angled the phone toward me and I watched, delighted, as she blocked his number. Then, as quickly as she'd done it, she asked me what I thought about the kanpachi.

THE HOLLYWOOD ENDING

"Do you want to hold her?" The nurse who'd wanted to make small talk before my C-section placed Rochelle in my arms before I could answer.

I felt some of the worst pain I'd ever sustained until this moment, but as I stared into my baby's eyes, I knew: I'd dedicated my entire career to finding other people love, but now I was experiencing a different form of it entirely. This concept of feeling pain to appreciate pleasure was a common one for athletes. After intense physical exertion, opioids—a neurochemical released in response to pain—are produced, often resulting in a feeling of euphoria (something known as a "runner's high"). Maybe that's what heartache was all about: embracing some degree of it to be able to fully cherish love. While I don't think heartache is an inevitability, it doesn't have to be in vain.

As I reflected on what brought me to this moment—a passion for my work, my husband, and now my child—I realized that none of it would have been possible without the love I had for myself. I can't always find someone's perfect match, but I know deep down that if I can help someone find *themselves*, the rest will follow.

"Rocky! It's time to blow out the candles!" I summoned my pigtailed toddler to the gazebo at the playground, where all her friends and family had gathered to wish her a happy birthday. Dave picked her up, and I lightly held back her arms, not wanting a repeat of the year before when she tried touching the candle's flame.

As everyone sang, the moment felt surreal. After all, it wasn't that long ago when we believed a day like today might never come. I looked around at the sea of smiling faces and small children running around, and decided to take a mental snapshot I could revisit anytime in the future. Then, off in the distance, I thought I glimpsed a familiar face.

"Everything okay?" Dave asked quietly, noticing my wandering gaze.

"Yeah, yeah, of course."

But as Rocky devoured her slice of cake and ran off toward the slide with her Mom Mom, I had to find out whether my mind was playing tricks on me. As I slowly approached the woman sitting on the bench, I saw that she was resting her hand on what appeared to be her belly.

"Callie?" She smiled at me widely, seeming not at all thrown by my presence. "Oh my gosh, how are you? You're—" I glanced at her baby bump, not wanting to mistakenly assume anything. But still, it appeared to be quite obvious.

"Yes." She laughed at my awkwardness. "I'm pregnant."

I wanted to tell her how worried I'd been years ago when she hadn't shown up for that final, complimentary coaching session. But instead I simply said, "You're glowing."

"Thanks! Here, sit." She slid over and indicated the spot beside her. I obliged. "Is that you over there?" She gestured to the sectioned-off area on the playground with balloons and a face painter.

"My daughter just turned two. She's super into Peppa Pig," I referred to the obvious theme of the party.

"So's my son!" she shared. "He's obsessed!" She smiled, sensing my confusion. "Sage?" She called out to a little boy around Rocky's age who was playing with her and my mom by the slide. As he bounded toward us, I recognized the distinguishable wispy brown hair, along with a calm, confident energy, and it took everything in me not to cry happy tears. The kid she'd always wanted was barely older than Rocky!

"Callie, wow. Does this mean—"

"Yup." She grinned. "I didn't do IVF, though. At least not the first time. I mean, I totally would have, since you failed to find me a husband and all."

My face fell, completely missing her sarcasm. "Kidding, kidding!" she quickly added. "I got knocked up the good ol'-fashioned way, right after our last session actually." *So that was it*, I thought. *No death in the family or poorly set alarm clock. She had met someone.* "It worked out for the best, though."

Sage approached before I could ask any questions, and tugged at his mom's pant leg. "Mommy, Peppa?" He stared in the direction of Rocky's British-pig-themed party.

"Go ahead, check it out!" I encouraged Sage, who ran full speed toward the festivities. "Callie, he's adorable."

"You'd like his dad, I think. I can't believe we're already on baby number two." She smiled jovially. "Kinda backwards, I suppose."

"Order, schmorder." I shrugged. "Are you happy?" Callie nodded. "That's all that matters then."

She told me her partner was a five-foot-seven TV writer. When I'd set her up, she didn't let me introduce her to any writers, let alone anyone "short." In fact, she'd hardly let me introduce her to anyone at all! Still, I wondered whether any of our conversations had played a role in helping her connect with him. Like with most of my clients, I'd probably never find out, but I supposed that wasn't the point.

"I was such a bozo back then," Callie acknowledged to me. "I don't know how you do it."

Sometimes, I wasn't sure either. But on days like today, I certainly knew *why*.

Acknowledgments

To my incredible husband, Dave, my muse and forever match, whose sacrifices from the time we met helped make this dream possible. Your unwavering support, dedication, and belief in our aspirational love story make waking up every day an exciting new adventure. To my miracle Rochelle, who makes me feel complete in a way I never knew was possible: You're destined to change the world one day. You've forever changed mine. To my mom: The first editor I ever had, who knew this day would come long before I did. Your unconditional love and embodiment of true grit make you the ultimate yellow canary. To my dad, whose unrelenting idealism I seem to have inherited: I'll carry your selflessness, resilience, and strength with me always. To my brother Jordan, whose impartiality, humility, and generosity keep our family going, and to my brother Josh, who somehow manages to be the quiet voice of reason while still being the loudest voice in the room. Your contributions don't go unnoticed.

To the Kuba and Silverberg families for their indispensable encouragement. May everyone be as blessed as I am to marry into families like theirs. To the Sherrin and Mahalec families for providing the breath of fresh air used to finish this impassioned endeavor. Your beautiful haven on Asilomar Boulevard in the Palisades will live on in my memory for life.

To my friends Flor, Jackie, Katie, and Andrea for their insight and always knowing exactly what to say at the times I needed to hear it most. You women are forces to be reckoned with, and are constantly inspiring me. And to Kate, who suffered through early reads and provided invaluable notes. Your book is next!

To Tony Jaswinski for teaching me college-level grammar in the seventh and eighth grade, so that I didn't totally embarrass myself with my publisher. To Lori Gottlieb, whose memoir *Maybe You Should Talk to Someone* gave me something to strive for.

To my fellow matchmakers, whom I continue to learn from daily, you paved a path that aroused something in my soul, and helped me find my identity. To Lauren Rosenberg, the yin to my yang, for sharing my vision about making the world a better place. I've loved partaking in this crazy adventure with you.

To my clients, those who lent their words to this book and otherwise, I'm invested in each and every one of your journeys, and want your love stories to work out as well as my own did.

To Laura Gordon and Mollie Glick for seeing the book's potential so early in the process. To Carolyn Kelly and Julianna Haubner, my darling mind readers and magicians, for making an otherwise tedious process both seamless and exciting. Carolyn, your professionalism and talent carried me through. To Abby Walters, my champion, without whom this book would not have been possible. I'm forever indebted to you for your belief in me and masterful ability to talk me off a ledge. To Peter Jarvis, my other champion, to whom I owe one killer adaptation. And to Jofie Ferrari-Adler, who proved that one chance encounter can truly change your life.

About the Author

JAYDI SAMUELS KUBA got her start in television writing, with credits on shows ranging from *Family Guy* to *Salem*. After watching her colleagues in film and TV struggle to find meaningful relationships, she helped launch LJMatchmaking, a couple-curation service for people in the industry. The dozens of power couples she has helped to introduce affectionately call her and her business partner the "Love Agents of Hollywood." A certified dating and relationship coach, Jaydi resides in Los Angeles with her daughter and her husband, with whom she cohosts the podcast *Match Made in Hollywood*.

Avid Reader Press, an imprint of Simon & Schuster, is built on the idea that the most rewarding publishing has three common denominators: great books, published with intense focus, in true partnership. Thank you to the Avid Reader Press colleagues who collaborated on *Your Last First Date*, as well as to the hundreds of professionals in the Simon & Schuster advertising, audio, communications, design, ebook, finance, human resources, legal, marketing, operations, production, sales, supply chain, subsidiary rights, and warehouse departments whose invaluable support and expertise benefit every one of our titles.

Editorial
Carolyn Kelly, *Editor*

Jacket Design
Alison Forner, *Senior Art Director*
Clay Smith, *Senior Designer*
Sydney Newman, *Art Associate*

Marketing
Meredith Vilarello, *VP and Associate Publisher*
Caroline McGregor, *Senior Marketing Manager*
Katya Wiegmann, *Marketing and Publishing Assistant*

Production
Allison Green, *Managing Editor*
Hana Handzjia, *Managing Editorial Assistant*
Samantha Hoback, *Senior Production Editor*
Alicia Brancato, *Production Manager*
Ruth Lee-Mui, *Interior Text Designer*
Cait Lamborne, *Ebook Developer*

Publicity
Ilana Gold, *Publicity Director*
Eva Kerins, *Publicity Assistant*
Lily Soroka, *Publicity Assistant*

Publisher
Jofie Ferrari-Adler, *VP and Publisher*

Subsidiary Rights
Paul O'Halloran, *VP and Director of Subsidiary Rights*
Fiona Sharp, *Subsidiary Rights Coordinator*